PAGANISM

AND PAGAN SURVIVALS IN SPAIN

UP TO THE FALL OF THE VISIGOTHIC

KINGDOM

Stephen McKenna

PREFACE

The purpose of the present study is to describe the struggle against paganism and pagan survival in Spain up to the fall of the Visigothic kingdom in 712. By paganism is here meant not only the worship of the pagan gods, but also the practices associated with pagan worship, such as astrology and magic. An attempt will be made to show the part that political, social and religious factors played in pagan survivals as well as to point out the various manifestations of paganism. This study, it is hoped, will throw light upon a phase of early Spanish history that has not hitherto been adequately treated. It will enable the reader to compare the paganism of Spain with that found in Africa, France, Germany and Italy, in as far as the extant sources and modern studies make such comparison possible.

In Spain as elsewhere in the empire the legislation of Constantine and Licinius marked a revolutionary change in the policy of the Roman government toward religion. Theoretically Christianity was now placed on an equal footing with paganism, but in practice from the first Constantine favored Christianity. Paganism steadily declined under the Christian emperors. The short pagan reaction brought about by Julian had no lasting effect and by the end of the fourth century pagan worship was definitely proscribed. But while the official pagan cults were easily suppressed the private practice of paganism offered a stubborn resistance to the progress of Christianity. The invasion of the empire by the Germanic peoples in the fourth and fifth centuries tended to keep alive pagan practices, for these invaders were either pagans or Arians and their hostility to the Catholics of the empire forced the Church in many places to struggle for its very existence. It was only after the conversion of the barbarians to Catholicism that successful efforts could be made against the paganism that still survived in the regions of the empire occupied by the barbarian peoples.

For a proper understanding of the subject it is necessary to give a survey of the pagan religions that existed in the Spanish Peninsula prior to the triumph of Christianity. Our knowledge of these pagan beliefs and practices is derived from the inscriptions and archaeological remains dating from the period of the empire and occasional references to the religion of the Spanish people in Greek and Latin writers. Full use has been made of the chief modern works that deal with paganism in Spain, in particular J. Toutain, *Les cultes paiens dans l'empire romain,* and Leite de Vasconcellos, *Religiões da Lusitania.* The writer has supplemented the studies of these two men by utilizing the discoveries on the early religions of Spain that have been made since their works were published. He has also made a special effort to show the localities in Spain where the pagan cults flourished and the probable influence which they had on the people of the Peninsula.

A comprehensive treatment of paganism in Spain down to the end of the third century A.D. forms the subject matter of the first chapter. The second chapter carries this history down from the council of Elvira, held about the year 306, to the Germanic invasions of Spain at the beginning of the fifth century. The canons of Elvira not only give us an insight into the organization of the Spanish Church, but also reveal the attitude of the ecclesiastical authorities to the paganism that surrounded them. For the rest of the fourth century the chief source is the anti-pagan legislation of the Christian emperors as found in the Theodosian Code.

A chapter has been devoted to Priscillianism, since this heresy, besides causing dissension in the Spanish hierarchy for almost two hundred years, perpetuated a number of superstitious beliefs and practices among the people. Only those problems in connection with Priscillianism have been studied that enable the reader to secure a better understanding of the pagan practices that were associated with it.

The fourth chapter contains a full analysis of the *De correctione rusticorum* of St. Martin of Braga, our most important source on the history of paganism in Spain in the sixth century. While the introduction and notes to Caspari's edition of this sermon published in 1883 are very valuable, many important features of Martin's attitude toward paganism have been overlooked and Caspari's explanation of many practices needed to be revised in the light of more recent studies. The closing chapter deals with the survivals of paganism in Visigothic Spain. As the relatively large number of writers in this kingdom, with one or two exceptions, give practically no information on the pagan survivals of their region in the sixth and seventh centuries, our knowledge of paganism there must be gleaned mainly from the Visigothic Code and the conciliar legislation. Finally, considerable attention has been given to the efforts of the Church at dispelling ignorance among the clergy and people and to the exorcisms and blessings of the Mozarabic rite as factors in counteracting and supplanting pagan beliefs and practices.

The writer takes this opportunity to thank his religious superiors for the privilege of continuing his studies at the Graduate School of the Catholic University of America. To his professors at the University he is also deeply grateful. He owes a special debt of gratitude to the Reverend Doctor Aloysius K. Ziegler and to Doctor Martin R. P. McGuire for the help and guidance received from them in writing the present dissertation.

Mount Saint Alphonsus,
Esopus, New York,
January, 1938.

CHAPTER ONE

Paganism and Christianity in Spain Before the Council of Elvira

To understand the pagan practices that survived in early Christian Spain it is necessary to make a study of the paganism that existed in the Peninsula before the coming of Christianity. Hence this opening chapter will be devoted to a rapid survey of the various peoples that settled there and a more detailed account of their religious beliefs and practices.

THE PEOPLES THAT SETTLED IN SPAIN

The earliest history of Spain like that of most countries is very obscure. According to A. Schulten, the first inhabitants of the Peninsula were probably the Ligurians, for a long period the principal people of western Europe. Only a few facts are known about their origin, their language, and the extent of their settlement. The assertion of some historians that the Ligurians and the Iberians were two branches of the same race is unfounded.

The Iberians are known to have been in Spain about the year 700 B.C., though doubtless they had come there much earlier. Their origin is a matter of dispute. Schulten, Gsell, Bosch-Gimpera claim that the Iberians came from Africa. Between this people and the pre-Celtic inhabitants of Ireland there seems to have been a very close connection. In early Ireland and Spain the bodies of the deceased were often dismembered; this unusual burial practice argues for a similarity of civilization if not of race. The writing on the famous Clonfinloch stone of Ireland is strikingly similar to that found on the walls in some places of southern Spain. The Iberians were the most important people to settle in Spain; they gave their name to the Peninsula and to the important river, the Iberus (Ebro).

Probably between the years 700-500 B.C. a new people, the Celts, entered Spain. Their first settlements were in the table-lands of central and northern Spain; later they brought the greater part of the western coast under their control. Their presence in this latter section is attested by many places with the Celtic ending *briga*, such, as Conimbriga (Coimbra), Caesarobriga (Talavera de la Reina), and Caetobriga (Setúbal).

Probably about the year 400 B. C. the Iberians of Provence invaded Spain and conquered the Celts in the table-lands and along the western coast. The Iberians who settled in the table-lands were known as the Celt-Iberians to distinguish them from the Iberians in other parts of Spain. Though the Celts were conquered, their influence did not die out entirely. The weapons used by the Celt-Iberians, the clothing that they wore, and the deities that they worshiped testify to the presence of the Celts in this locality. But the system of government adopted by the Celt-Iberians, their manner of waging war, and their traits of character are certainly Iberian.

The vast mineral wealth of Spain, tin, copper and silver, became known at an early date to the Phoenicians who had preceded the Iberians and the Celts to Spain. About the year 1000 B.C. they established a trading post at Gades (Cadiz), which later became one of the most important cities of early Spain.-They gained control of a large portion of southern Spain, and probably established settlements at Tartessus, Agadir and Belon. To the tribes of southern Spain they brought the benefits of a higher civilization and probably taught them the alphabet.

In the eighth or seventh century B.C. the Greeks began to trade with the tribes of southern Spain and along the Mediterranean coast. In the fourth century B.C. they made settlements in northeastern Spain. Colonies were founded at Emporion (Castellon de Ampurias) and Rhodus (Rosas) by the Greeks, but no settlements were made by them in southeastern Spain.

After the Carthaginians in the sixth century B.C. had firmly established their position in North Africa they invaded Spain and gradually gained control of the Phoenician settlements there. While the history of the Carthaginians in Spain is very obscure at this early period, they seem to have founded colonies at Nova Carthago (Cartagena), Malaca (Málaga) and at other places along the Mediterranean coast. It was not until the time of Hamilcar, Hasdrubal and Hannibal in the third century B.C. that the Carthaginians pushed their conquests into western Spain. They never succeeded in subduing a number of the tribes of Cantabria and modern Portugal.

The Romans did not enter Spain before the Punic Wars of the third century B.C. During the Second Punic War Spain played an important part, and the victories which the Roman armies won there ultimately sealed the doom of Carthage. The Romans now began a systematic conquest of the Spanish tribes, and most of Spain was definitely under their control after the fall of Numantia in 133 B.C. It was more than a century later before the fierce tribes of Cantabria submitted to the Roman yoke. Rome remained in control of the Peninsula until the invasion of the Germanic peoples four centuries later. The history of Spain under the empire was very peaceful and Roman civilization gradually penetrated throughout the Peninsula.

NATIVE RELIGIONS OF SPAIN

Just as the history of the early Ligurians, Iberians and Celts in Spain is very obscure, so little is known about their primitive religious beliefs. For example, did the Druids, who in the time of Caesar were the religious leaders of the Celts of Gaul, ever come to Spain? None of the ancient Greek and Roman writers of Spanish history mention their presence in the Peninsula. H. Hubert thinks that the Druids may have been known there by a different name. But from the words of Caesar that Druidism came from Britain and that those who wished to become Druids went there to study, J. Pokorny, H. d'Arbois de Jubainville and G. Dottin conclude that Druidism was a pre-Celtic institution, which the Celts adopted after their conquest of Britain. As Druidism did not in all probability exist in Spain, the fusion of the Iberians and the Celts could be accomplished more easily and doubtless in the course of time many changes were made in the religion of both peoples. It will therefore be necessary to discuss the Iberian and Celtic religions as if they were but one.

Greek and Roman writers seldom mention the religious beliefs of the early inhabitants of Spain and this lack of source material makes the study of the native cults of Spain less satisfactory than that of the neighboring peoples of Africa and Gaul. It is true that beginning with the first century of the Christian era, there are many inscriptions to the native gods. But, as the inscriptions in themselves do not furnish details about the worship that was practiced, there are some difficult problems which have not yet been solved. For example, should the names of such deities as *A biafelaesurraecus, Ahoparaligomenus* and *Crougintoudadigoa* be spelled as one word or several words? In many cases only the name of the god or goddess is given. On some of the inscriptions to the native gods there are words written in a native language, which still puzzles the investigators.

For the sake of clarity the more important deities will be discussed first, and then the less prominent gods and goddesses (those worshiped on mountain tops, in the rivers, the fountains, and at the sacred stones). This will be followed by a list of the deities, whose names only are known to us, and the places where inscriptions to them have been found.

The most noted of the native deities of Spain was Endovellicus. About fifty inscriptions have been found on which his name is mentioned. The center of his cult seems to have been near the city of Ebora (Evora) in modern Portugal. There have been various attempts to explain the meaning of the name of this deity, but the etymologies are merely arbitrary. Endovellicus is sometimes invoked as the god of health; in other inscriptions he is addressed as the *Deus Sanctus* or the *Numen praesentissimum et praestantissimum*. Most of the inscriptions to Endovellicus have been found on a high hill, and hence Leite de Vasconcellos concludes that he was the god who protected the locality in which he was usually invoked.

To Ataecina, a female deity, about twenty inscriptions have been found. Her cult was more widespread than that of Endovellicus, for the inscriptions appear in various parts of southern Portugal and in western Andalusia. The frequent shortening of her name on the inscriptions indicates her widespread popularity. Ataecina is identified, for example, with the Greco-Roman goddess Proserpina, who was looked upon as an agrarian deity, and as the queen of Hades presiding over the region of the dead. She is addressed in the inscriptions as *Sancta, Domina, Servatrix* and *Invicta*. In an inscription at Merida this goddess is requested to recover some clothes which have been stolen. Ataecina was probably a Celtic deity, though her name is not found in other countries where the Celts had settled.

Besides Endovellicus a number of other deities appear to have been invoked on the tops of mountains. In a mountain near Braga called Distertius (Distercio) an inscription was found to Dercetius, presumably the god of the mountain. St. Aemilian, who lived in the sixth century A. D., later retired to this mountain. Here, according to St. Braulio, his seventh century biographer, he experienced the "mockeries of the ancient scoundrel"– who, Toutain surmises, was the god Dercetius. Two ex-votos have been found in the mountains of this same section to the gods Brigus and Cabuniaegenis At times the cult of Jupiter is associated with that of a native god. Thus *Iuppiter Ladicus* appears to have been invoked on the mountain near Lugo, which is today called Ladoco. *Iuppiter Candamius* was, according to Hübner, the deity who presided over the mountain near Astorga, now known as

Candanedo.

There are clear traces of the worship of rivers, especially in northern and western Spain. An inscription has been found to the god Durius, who presided probably over the river of this same name, Durius (Douro). To the north of this same river near the city of Bracara (Braga) the names of the gods, Tameobrigus and Durbeicus have been found. It has been suggested that these gods watched over the rivers known today as Tamaio and Avo. Five inscriptions to the goddess Nabia have been discovered. She was probably a river deity and her name lives on in the river Navia of northern Spain.

The divinities who watched over fountains seem to have been especially dear to the natives of Spain. An inscription found upon a fountain outside of the city of Bracara (Braga) is dedicated to the god Tongoenabiacus. On the stone above the fountain is the picture of a person standing who holds in his left arm what appears to be a basket of fruit. Toutain suggests that this is a picture of the fountain-god Tongoenabiacus and that he is supposed to bring fertility to the country-side. Around Guimarens, still famous for its mineral water, two inscriptions have been found to the god Bormanicus. Whether he was a Celtic or Ligurian deity is still a matter of dispute. The *Nymphae* were often invoked as the goddesses of fountains. This cult was pre-Roman, as is evident from the fact that most of the inscriptions to the Nymphs have been found in western and northwestern Spain. Dedications to the deity that watches over the fountain are found in such formulas as *Aquae Eletes,* west of Salmantica, and *Fons Saginiesis*, near Astorga.

The worship of the *Lar* and *Genius* in Spain is frequently in the last analysis a native cult, as is clear from the epithets applied to them. Thus at Capera (el Villar) there is an inscription to the *Lares Gapeticorum Gentilitatis*. There are also inscriptions to the *Lares Turolici, Cerenaeci, Cusicelenses*. In these same sections of western and northwestern Spain the Roman *Genii, Dii* and *Lares,* were often invoked as the protectors of the towns, localities and travelers, as the *Dii Deaeque Coniumbricenses, Genius Turgalesium, Genius Laquiniesis* and *Lares viales.*

The natives of Spain regarded many rocks and stones as sacred. Thus among the inscriptions to Endovellicus is one which reads as follows: *"Endovolico Iulia Anas relictum a Majoribus Animo Libens Posuit."* The words *relictum a majoribus* refer probably to the stone itself, which was sacred in the family of Julia, and hence was worthy of being offered to Endovellicus. Even in the worship of the fountain-deity, Tongoenabiacus, the essential part of the worship was the stone above the fountain on which the name and probably also the image of the god were engraved. The most curious of all these sacred stones is one found near Braga. The inscription is as follows: *"Diis Deabusque Aeternum Lacum Omnibusque Numinibus Lapitearum cum hoc templo sacravit . . . in quo hostiae voto cremantur."* The word *templum* in this inscription probably designates the stone itself upon which the victim was burnt. It may have been at one of these sacred stones that the Lusitanians sacrificed their prisoners of war to one of their gods by cutting off their right hands and inflicting upon them other tortures.

On the promontory of St. Vincent, which in ancient times was thought to be the most western point of the inhabited world, some stones were also regarded as sacred. Strabo says that the natives were wont to turn these stones about and pour an oblation on them. And he adds: "It is not lawful to offer sacrifices at this place, nor at night even to set foot on the promontory because, as the people say, the gods occupy it at this time." Even at the present time the people avoid visiting the cape at night. Probably there existed the belief, not uncommon among primitive people, that the souls of the dead dwelt in certain stones which, when turned about, were capable of producing rain.

The other deities, worshiped by the native Celts and Iberians, were local gods and goddesses about whom only the name is known. There are about eighty of these deities. In the following list they are arranged according to the locality in which inscriptions to them have been found. The symbol * denotes that the name of the deity is uncertain.

Astorga -- Aernus, Ameuncus, Bodus, Caraedudis, Coso, *Degante, Mamdica, *Menoviacus, Vaccaburius, Vagdonnaegus.

Braga -- Abiafelaesurraecus, Abna, Aegiamunniaegus, Ameipicer, Banderaeicus, Bandua, Bandueaetobrigus, Bmervasecus,　Bormanicus, *Cabar, *Castaecae, Cauleces, *Coronus, Cusicelenses, Cusuneneaecus, Durbedicus, Durius, *Frovida, Nabia, *Netaci, *Ocaere, *Saur, Tameobrigus, Turolici, Turiacus.

Cáceres -- Angefix, Arentius, Bandoga, Bcantunaecus, Bidiesis, *Boutes, Caparenses, *Eaecus, Labarus, Macer, Reuveanabaraecus, Runesius Cesius, Silonsaclo, *Saga, Suttunius, Tiauranceaicus, Toga, Tribarone.

Lisbon -- *Aracus, Bandiarbariaicus, *Carneus, Coniumbricenses.

Lugo -- Ahoparaliomegus, *Caulex, Crougintoudadigoa, Cuhueberralagecu, Edovius, *Obiane, Regoni, *Verore.

Saragossa -- Obana, Stelatesa.

Toledo -- Aelmanius, Leiossa, Lougiae, Lumiae, *Mogoninon, Pindusa, *Togoti, Varcilenae.

Uncertain Places -- Ceceaigi, *Falcus, *Salogu.

One hundred and thirty native deities are known to us by name, and there are about 230 inscriptions dedicated to them. As is evident from what has been shown above, the center of these native cults was in western and northwestern Spain. In the other parts of Spain there are no dedications to the native gods and goddesses. This does not mean that Rome had forbidden the people to worship them, but merely that the aborigines of southern and eastern Spain had adopted not merely the civilization, but also the religion of the Romans.

Whether these deities are Celtic, Iberian or even Ligurian is still an open question. Those gods whose names end in *aecus* and *aegus* seem to be Iberian. The deities that are undoubtedly of Celtic origin, as the *Matres, Lugoves,* and *Epona,* the goddess of horses, are found near Clunia (Coruña del Conde) where some of the Celt-Iberians are known to have settled. Occasionally a group of people dedicates an inscription to the native deities, as that made by the *collegium sutorum* to the *Lugoves,* but as a rule most of the inscriptions are made by private individuals. The large number of these deities and the inscriptions to them prove their popularity among the people. As far as can be judged, the Roman civil and military officials in western and northwestern Spain seldom make any inscription to the native gods. The only exception appears to be that made by the city of Astorga to Vagdonnaegus. While the names of soldiers are on some of these inscriptions to the native deities, Toutain surmises that they were probably natives of Spain in the service of Rome.

When did the cult of these native deities come to an end? Toutain believes that there is no means of knowing if their worship was practiced in the third and fourth century of the Christian era. But he has overlooked the fact that as late as the fifth, sixth and seventh centuries many people of Spain were condemned by the missionaries and councils for the superstitious rites which they practiced at the fountains and stones.

THE RELIGION OF THE PHOENICIANS IN SPAIN

Besides the cults of the natives of Spain, the Phoenicians, Greeks and Romans who settled there left an appreciable influence upon the religious life of the Peninsula. With the religion of the Phoenicians may be linked that of the Carthaginians, for the two people worshiped the same gods and had the same religious beliefs. Among the Phoenicians there was in each locality a deity known by the general name of Baal, whose power was limited to the place in which he was worshiped. In the city of Gades (Cadiz) there were two temples to Cronus and Melkarth (= "king of the city").The god, *Hercules Gaditanus,* probably a Latinized form of Melkarth, was very popular among the Romans, and his name is often found on the coins used in Roman times. There are no extant remains of the Phoenician temples at Cadiz. Toutain has called attention to the fact that in Roman times there were in Africa and Spain many dedications to the *Genius municipii.* As most of the places where these inscriptions have been found had formerly been settlements of the Phoenicians he concludes that the worship of the local Baal of the Phoenicians continued under the Roman name of *Genius municipii.*

THE RELIGION OF THE GREEKS IN SPAIN

In the northeastern section of Spain, where the Greeks had established three colonies, the Greek cults were introduced at an early date. Strabo is authority for the statement that even the natives of these sections began to worship the goddess Artemis in the manner of the Greeks.- Recent excavations made in the ancient city of Emporion have brought to light the remains of a temple to Asclepius and of a statue to Artemis. A number of other cults containing Greek elements were introduced later by the Romans and hence are treated in the next section.

THE RELIGION OF THE ROMANS IN SPAIN

The religion brought to Spain by the Romans is better known than that of the native, the Phoenician, and the Greek cults. Through centuries of settlement and administration the Romans exerted a tremendous influence upon the religious life of the Peninsula. The religion of Rome was spread throughout Spain by the army veterans and the Italians who settled there beginning with the second century B. C. But unfortunately we know almost nothing about the Roman cults in Spain before the empire. For convenience of treatment the Roman religion may be divided into the official and non-official cults. In the discussion of the official cults the plan of presentation adopted by Toutain– will be followed, and in the non-official cults that by Wissowa.

The purpose of the official cults was to honor the emperor as the head of the state. This worship had been started in Spain during the life-time of Augustus. During the war against the Cantabrians about 25 B. C. the people in the Romanized city of Tarraco (Tarragona) had built an altar in honor of the emperor. This worship of the ruler that began so spontaneously became very popular in the Romanized sections of the Peninsula.

This popularity is evident from the fact that in Spain not only each province, but also each *conventus* (a juridical district embracing a certain number of towns), and very often each municipality had its own imperial cult. The writer has examined the Spanish inscriptions on which are found the names of *flamines, flaminicae* and *sevirales,* who were closely associated with the imperial cult. In thirty-four towns of Baetica there is mention made in thirty-four inscriptions of the *flamines,* in eighteen of the *flaminicae,* and in thirty-four of the *sevirales.* In nine towns of Lusitania the *flamines* are mentioned ten times, the *flaminicae* eight times, and the *sevirales* eight times. In forty-five towns of Tarraconensis the *flamines* are mentioned sixty-five times, the *flaminicae* ten times, and the *sevirales* twenty-four times.

While the worship of the reigning emperor was the principal part of the imperial cult, Tiberius, as far as is known, is the only emperor mentioned by name in Spain. Occasionally there are inscriptions to the *Numen* or the *Lares* of the emperor. More frequently the cult of Augustus (the name by which the ruling emperor was usually known) was associated with that of other divinities. But the most popular form of the imperial cult in Spain was undoubtedly that of the *divi*.

In Spain the priest in charge of the imperial cult was generally given the title *flamen divorum et Augustorum*. This cult of *all* the *divi* is the more striking when it is remembered that it was not practiced elsewhere in the Roman world. A special priest in Spain was appointed to conduct the worship of each *divus*. Later when the women of the imperial household were declared *divae* a special priestess presided over the worship paid to them. While in other parts of the empire the oath which the civil official took mentioned as a rule only the reigning emperor, at Malaca (Málaga), and probably elsewhere in Spain the *divi* were also included. The oath taken by the officials of this city was in part as follows: "Facito ut is iuret per Iovem et divom Augustum et divom Claudium et divom Vespasianum Augustum et divom Titum Augustum et genium Caesaris Domitiani Augustes deosque Penates..." This popularity of the cult of the *divi* was due very probably to the fact that when the Emperor Augustus had been declared a *divus* the people of Tarraconensis had asked and obtained permission from Tiberius to have a temple built in honor of the departed emperor. This action of Tarraconensis set an example to the other Spanish provinces.

The official cult also included the worship of the capitoline deities, *Iuppiter Optimus Maximus, Iuno* and *Minerva*. This cult spread throughout the provinces and in Spain, it is known to have been formally established at Hispalis (Seville) and Urso (Orsuna).

Only five inscriptions in Spain have been found in which the three capitoline deities have been invoked together, and the occasions of these inscriptions seem to have been events of public interest. Juno is invoked on fifteen inscriptions in Spain and in four of them the title *Regina* is added. Minerva is sometimes invoked alone, and on four inscriptions she is called *Augusta.* The most popular of the three deities was undoubtedly *Iuppiter Optimus Maximus,* or *I.O.M.,* as his name was usually abbreviated. Eighty-seven inscriptions have been found on which this name is mentioned.

The names of the natives of Spain are occasionally found on these inscriptions to the capitoline deities in which they are invoked separately, but not on those in which their names are joined together. Civil officials and freedmen, often with Greek names, predominate in the cult of Juno and Minerva. In the inscriptions to *I.O.M.* are to be found the names of slaves, freedmen and civil officials But this cult of Jupiter as the head of the State was especially fostered by the soldiers in Spain. More than half of the inscriptions to him have been found near Braga and Lugo, where the *Legio VII Gemina* was stationed.

NON-OFFICIAL CULTS

Besides the cult paid to the Capitoline Jupiter, there was also the worship of Jupiter as the lord of the world. The evidence for this cult is seen in the inscriptions which are not followed by the words *Capitolinus* or *Optimus Maximus.* Jupiter enjoyed an especial popularity in Lusitania, for most of the Spanish inscriptions mentioning Jupiter are found there. On these inscriptions he is usually called *Solutorius,* which was probably a corruption of *Salutaris* Jupiter was identified, as has been pointed out, with the native gods *Ladicus* and *Candamius.* Doubtless *Celtius Tongi f.* who dedicated an inscription to *Iuppiter Repulsor,* associated the worship of the Roman god with a native deity.

Next to Jupiter, Mars was probably the most popular Roman deity worshiped in Spain. There are more than forty inscriptions to him. As has been already pointed out, the name Mars is often followed by that of Augustus. The Roman god is sometimes called *Pater, Invictus, Campester.* In an inscription found at Tuy, near Braga, the name of a native god *Caniociecus* is added to that of Mars. Perhaps the name of the god Cosus was also connected with Mars in an inscription found at Brandomil, near Coruña, in Galicia. This proves that a native cult corresponding to that of Mars already existed in Spain before the coming of the Romans. But whatever modification the cult of Mars received in a Spanish environment the Italian names on a number of inscriptions to Mars, as Vettila Paculi, Cominius, Vibius Persinus, and Arruntius Initialis, seem to indicate that the old Roman cult as such was transplanted to Spain.

Juno was invoked in Spain as one of the heavenly deities. This cult of Juno Caelestis was probably Semitic in origin. Not far from Cartagena a temple had been built in her honor.

Neptune, the god of the sea, was especially honored in the seaport towns of Cadiz and Tarragona. While in Africa and Gaul Neptune was often invoked as a fountain-deity, there do not seem to have been any fountains in Spain which were dedicated to him.

Four inscriptions have been found in Spain to Silvanus, which Toutain has overlooked in his discussion of this Roman god. Silvanus seems to have preserved in the Peninsula his Roman character as the god who watches over the fields.

Tutela was probably the most popular abstract conception that was worshiped in Spain. Sometimes the name *Tutela* is found alone, but more often the formula is met, *Tutela colonorum Cluniensium,* or *Genius Tutela horreorum.* All of the fourteen inscriptions in Spain have been found in western Tarraconensis. Three towns of the Peninsula have derived their names from *Tutela*: Tudela Vegún near León, Tudela de Duero near Valladolid, and Tudela not far from Saragossa.

At Saguntum (Sagunto) there was a temple dedicated to Diana, and in this same city there is found an inscription which speaks of the various animals that have been offered to her. In the northwestern section of Spain three inscriptions to her have been found as the patroness of hunters, *Diana Venatrix*.

Besides the cult of Minerva as a capitoline deity, she was also invoked in Spain under the Greek aspect as patroness of the trades. Most of the inscriptions to Minerva have been found in the Romanized sections of southern and eastern Spain. There were two temples built in her honor, one at Gades (Cadiz) and the other at Tarraco (Tarragona).

As was mentioned above the Phoenician god Melkarth was probably worshiped at Gades under the name of Hercules. The Greco-Roman Hercules was very popular in southern and eastern Spain where twenty inscriptions to him have been found. At Carteia (Rocadilo) and Epora (Montoro) not far from Gades, mention is made on the inscriptions of the "priests of Hercules."

About twelve inscriptions to Venus have been found in Spain. Her cult appears to have been popular in the southern and eastern parts of the Peninsula. In a number of these inscriptions, as has already been indicated, the name Augusta is added to that of Venus. In an inscription that has been recently found she is given the title *Victrix*.

Inscriptions have been found to Apollo in Lisbon, Braga, Valencia, and Cordova. In one inscription there is mention of Asclepius and Apollo, and near the modern town of Aroche in southern Spain there was a temple to Apollo and Diana. The names of the persons dedicating these inscriptions were apparently oriental, such as M. Afranius Euporius, Vibia Trophime, and Calpurnius Alypion.

Mercury was not as much honored in Spain as in Gaul, where the natives placed him first among the Roman deities. Only about fifteen inscriptions are known to have been dedicated to him. The center of his cult appears to have been at Cartagena where a temple had been built in his honor, and where the "fishermen and hucksters" dedicated a marble shaft to him.

At Cordova there was an inscription to the goddess Nemesis. In the city of Evora an inscription, which is undated, referred to the *"amici Nemesiaci."* Attention will be drawn to the "friends of Nemesis" in the following chapter.

Besides the above-mentioned deities which the Romans brought to Spain, there also came the worship of the gods of the dead, usually called *Dii Manes* or *Dii inferi Manes.-* On the tombs in Spain we also meet the common formula: "May the earth be light upon thee." Almost forty inscriptions to the Manes have been found in Spain. Though the majority of them have been found in the Romanized portions of the Peninsula, a number of inscriptions in northwestern Spain have also been discovered. It seems from the names on these inscriptions, as Alluquius Andergus, and Mineas Sato, that the natives of Spain had probably identified the Roman Manes with their own gods of the dead.

ORIENTAL MYSTERY RELIGIONS IN SPAIN

The last forms of paganism to enter Spain during the first three centuries after Christ were the oriental mystery cults. The first of these was the religion of Phrygia, whose great goddess was believed to have saved Rome from disaster during the war against Hannibal. The principal characteristic of this Phrygian cult was the *taurobolium* or *criobolium,* a ceremony which is also found in the religion of Mithras. This rite, which the Spanish poet Prudentius has described, consisted in the slaying of a bull or ram on an open platform. The neophytes who stood beneath the platform allowed the blood which flowed through the crevices to pour over the different parts of their body and often in their eagerness moistened their lips with it. A spiritual meaning was attached to this ceremony. The descent into the pit was regarded as a burial, and the sprinkling with blood signified the beginning of a new life.

While there were two principal deities of this Asiatic cult, Cybele and Attis, the latter is seldom mentioned in the Spanish inscriptions. Cybele was usually addressed as *Mater Deum.* An inscription in northwestern Spain identifies her with the Roman goddess Juno. In the Balearic Islands a temple was dedicated to *Mater Magna et Atthis* The inscriptions to the Phrygian deities are found in southern Lusitania and Baetica, in the northwestern section, and in the seaport town of Barcino (Barcelona). The names of many of the persons who dedicate these inscriptions are oriental, such as T. Licinius Amaranthus, Docyricus Valerianus, and Flavia Tyche. The earliest known inscription to *Magna Mater* in Spain was made in the year 108 A.D. The latest one that can be dated with certainty was made at Corduba (Cordova) about the year 238 A.D.

The Syrian cult of Atargatis seems to have been popular in southern Spain. Traces of this Syrian religion have been found at Cordova. An inscription found at Málaga refers to a settlement there of Syrian merchants who probably continued to worship the deities of their native land.

There are fourteen inscriptions to the Egyptian deities Isis and Serapis in Spain. While the title *Domina* is generally given to Isis, she is called in one inscription *Isidi puellari,* perhaps because she was regarded as the patroness of girls. An inscription discovered near a fountain may be an indication that Isis was regarded as a fountain-deity. An inscription to Isis at Corduba (Cordova) mentions the jewels and other precious ornaments which the worshiper offered to the goddess.- One inscription to Serapis joins his name with that of Jupiter. Another inscription addresses him as *Serapis Pantheus* Inscriptions in his honor are found in southern Lusitania, in Baetica, in northwestern Spain, and also along the Mediterranean coast, where there was a temple to Serapis at Emporion.

The inscriptions to these Egyptian deities are made by soldiers, slaves, or freedmen who have oriental names. At Valentia (Valencia) Isis is honored by the *sodalicium vernarum,* who may have been descendants of oriental slaves. Among the oriental names may be mentioned those of Flaminica Pale, Livia Chalcedonica, and Sempronia Lynchis. The only inscription that can be dated with certainty is that found at Corduba (Cordova) in the middle of the second century.

About twenty-five inscriptions to Mithras have been found in Spain. The center of his cult appears to have been at Merida where a number of statues to Mithras have been discovered. He was also worshiped at Tarragona, in parts of Baetica, and in the military sections of the northwest. Mithras is usually addressed as *Sol Dominus Invictus.* On an altar to him at Menda are engraved the words, *Ara Genesis Invicti Mithrae,* which probably refer to the birth of the god. The cult of Mithras appears to have been very popular in the middle of the second century A. D. Most of the inscriptions were made by soldiers.

The oriental mystery cults were popular in the maritime and military cities of Spain. No inscriptions to these eastern deities have been discovered in the central part of the Peninsula or in northwestern Lusitania. These religions did not make a deep impression upon the natives of Spain as may be judged from the fact that the names on the inscriptions are those of soldiers or of

24

people evidently oriental. The oriental religions led to the practice of magic and astrology in many countries of the West. While Toutain stresses the paucity of documents in Spain in regard to magic and astrology, he believes that Spain was permeated with magic.

There is evidence, however, that the syncretistic movement which had been going on in Roman religion from a very early period reached its culmination when the oriental cults entered the empire. This syncretism and its logical consequence, pantheism, are evident in the Spanish inscriptions. Mention has already been made of the frequency with which the Roman deities were associated with Cybele, Isis, and Mithras. In northwestern Spain, not far from Bracara (Braga) an altar was dedicated to more than twenty Greco-Roman deities. Some of the other inscriptions are made to *Iuppiter Pantheus Augustus, Pantheus Augustus, Serapis Pantheus,* and *Pantheus Tutela.* Five of these syncretistic inscriptions have been discovered in northwestern Spain and four in the province of Baetica. The other inscriptions are found in southern Lusitania and along the eastern coast.

CHRISTIANITY IN SPAIN BEFORE THE COUNCIL OF ELVIRA *(c.* 306)

The exact year in which Christianity came to Spain is a question that is impossible to settle from the extant evidence. There is no solid historical foundation for the claim that St. James preached the Gospel in Spain about the year 44 A.D. In his epistle to the Romans St. Paul had expressed the desire to evangelize Spain, and it seems probable from the words of St. Clement of Rome (*c.* 90 A. D.) and the Muratonian Fragment (*c.* 200 A.D.) that he actually carried this plan into effect. But if so there is nothing known about the place or the success of his labors. The story that SS. Peter and Paul sent seven missionaries to Spain is purely legendary. There are references to the existence of Christian churches in Spain in the writings of Irenaeus and Tertullian, both of whom wrote between the years 180 and 200 A.D., but evidence for the places in which Christianity was actually practiced comes only in the middle of the third century.

During the persecution of the Christians by the Emperor Decius in the years 249-251, the bishops of Legio-Asturica (León-Astorga) and Emerita (Merida), Basilides and Martial, had apostatized. Because such apostates could no longer retain their episcopal rank, the Christians in these towns had proceeded to elect others to fill the vacant Sees. Martial appealed to Pope Cornelius (253-255) and was reinstated. The people in their quandary turned to St. Cyprian, Bishop of Carthage, and other members of the African hierarchy. In his reply Cyprian after reviewing the accusations brought against Martial and Basilides, declared that the Christians of León-Astorga and Merida had acted justly in choosing men to succeed the apostates, and that the reinstated bishop was not entitled to the obedience of the laity and clergy. The sequel to this first glimpse into the history of the Church in Spain is unknown.

The next record of Christianity in Spain is to be found in the Valerian persecution (257-259). The only martyrs in Spain were Bishop Fructuosus of Tarragona and two deacons of this city, Eulogius and Augurius. From the account of the martyrdom of Fructuosus, which is generally regarded as authentic, it is evident that the Christians were already a strong minority in this city where the imperial cult had been deeply rooted. The martyred bishop, Fructuosus, was greatly beloved even by the pagans of Tarragona.

During the fifty years that followed the martyrdom of Fructuosus nothing is known about Christianity in Spain until the persecution of Diocletian (303-305). The names of about fifty martyrs during this persecution have come down to us. The places in which they were martyred were Corduba (Cordova), Calahorra (Calagurnis), Complutum (Alcalá de Henares), Emerita Augusta

26

(Merida), and Caesaraugusta (Saragossa). The best known of the eighteen martyrs of Saragossa is the deacon Vincent. At Merida there was martyred a young girl of twelve years named Eulalia, about whom an interesting discussion has recently been raised. G. Fliedner, the author of an article entitled, *"Das Weiterleben der Ataecina,"* calls attention to the fact that in pagan times the goddess Ataecina was very popular in the city of Merida and throughout the whole of Lusitania, and that in the same region in early Christian times Eulalia was held in high veneration. The same petitions, as Fliedner points out, are addressed to Ataecina and Eulalia. The titles given to Ataecina and Eulalia are somewhat similar. These facts are undeniable, but the conclusion which Fliedner draws that the honor paid to Eulalia was but a superstitious survival of the cult that had once been shown to Ataecina cannot be justified. A careful reading of the inscriptions to Ataecina clearly shows that the pagans regarded her as a deity. The Christians, on the contrary, are always aware of the fact that the favors which they have received, have come to them from God through the merits or intercession of Eulalia.

The facts, summarized in the above paragraphs, are all that is known about Christianity before the fourth century. As we learn from the Council of Elvira, however, communities of Christians were to be found at this time in Baetica, Carthaginiensis, eastern Tarraconensis, and also in the cities of the west and northwest. Probably also in some localities Christianity had penetrated into the country districts, where the churches were in charge of deacons. According to the *Adversus nationes* of Arnobius (written about 300) there were "innumerable Christians" living in Spain. While this statement may be exaggerated, the Church in Spain was in a flourishing condition, as is evident from the number of bishops at the Council of Elvira. The growth of the Spanish Church, aside from supernatural considerations, was due in part to the excellent roads which facilitated progress throughout the Peninsula, to the long peace which Spain enjoyed since the days of Augustus, and finally to the fact that in no other province of the empire were Roman institutions so deeply rooted as in the Iberian Peninsula.

During the course of the fourth century Christianity became triumphant in Spain. But even before the Edict of Toleration, which marked the beginning of this momentous change in the religious life of the empire, had been proclaimed, there took place the Council of Elvira, an epoch-making event in the Church-history of Spain. The canons of this council give the best extant knowledge of the paganism in Spain at the beginning of the year 306, and the attitude which the hierarchy of the country took toward it.

CHAPTER TWO

Paganism and Pagan Survivals in Spain During the Fourth Century

The period to which the present chapter is devoted is delimited by two important events in the history of the Spanish Peninsula. It begins with the Council of Elvira on the eve of the Edict of Toleration. The records of this important assembly, besides giving us our first idea concerning the organization of the Church in Spain, contain the reaction of the Catholics to the paganism which surrounded them. This council shows forth conditions as they were at the end of the period in which paganism enjoyed special privilege at the hands of the government. With the Edict of Toleration its position of privilege before the law was taken away and it was to enjoy only the religious liberty extended to all; soon it was to be proscribed. This period of roughly a hundred years was brought to an abrupt close and the development of culture in Spain was profoundly altered by the invasion of the barbarians at the beginning of the fifth century.

THE COUNCIL OF ELVIRA

The town of Elvira (Illiberis) where the bishops of Spain met was situated in the province of Baetica near the site of the present city of Granada. Practically all students of early Church history are agreed that the council was held before the Edict of Toleration

(313) and during the time when Constantius Chlorus was Caesar of the West (293-306). While some historians assert that the bishops met at Elvira before the persecution of Diocletian in Spain (303-305), internal evidence seems to indicate that the bishops assembled only after the persecution had ended, that is, about the year 306. Thus the council discussed the punishment to be meted out to informers *(delatores)*, to Christians who had sacrificed to the gods,- and also the question whether a person who had been killed in the act of destroying a pagan idol was entitled to the honors of martyrdom. Such problems were more likely to arise after a persecution than during a time when the Church was at peace.

Nineteen bishops attended the council, the most noted of them being Osius, who played such an important part in the ecclesiastical history of the subsequent period. All of the five provinces into which the Iberian Peninsula had been divided by Diocletian were represented at the council, and hence it may be called a "national" council. There was one bishop from Galicia and one from Tarraconensis; three bishops came from Lusitania, five from Carthaginiensis, and the remainder from Baetica. Twenty-four priests were also present, four of whom came from Carthaginiensis, and the other twenty from Baetica. Of the eighty-one canons which were enacted at Elvira, over twenty were concerned with paganism.

In the first canon the bishops declared that a member of the church who had worshiped an idol should not be admitted to "communion" even at the end of his life. Hefele thought that the word *"communio"* in these canons had the meaning of the Holy Eucharist. But the Latin *"communio"* seldom meant the Eucharist before the fourth century was well advanced. The more usual meaning was "communion with the Church," and a careful reading of the canons of Elvira indicates that the word is used in them in this sense. The council inflicted the penalty of perpetual exclusion from the Church for seventeen offenses. Rigorous though it was the severity of the bishops was not that of the Novatians, who denied that the Church had power to forgive sins committed after baptism. There are various other canons of Elvira which permit a sinner to return to the Church after he has performed the specified penance. This severe penalty of permanent excommunication, decreed by the bishops of Elvira, was perhaps the most effective means of preventing the faithful, living in the midst of a pagan society, from taking part in idolatrous worship and committing adultery and murder. The bishops were more lenient towards a catechumen *(christianus)* who had sacrificed to the gods and allowed him to be baptized after he had performed penance for ten years.

A problem closely connected with idolatry arose in regard to the Christian *flamines*. As was mentioned in the previous chapter, Spain had been very devoted to the imperial cult and in practically every town of any size there was to be found a priest who presided over the worship of the emperors. In practice civil and religious functions were inseparable in the pagan Roman administration and Christians could not hold office without coming in contact with the pagan religion as a part of their official duties. The bishops of Elvira were forced to express their attitude on the question whether a Christian could accept the office of *flamen* without giving up his membership in the Church. Three canons of the council dealt with this difficult problem. A Christian *flamen* who took part in the pagan sacrifices and in the "murder" and "immorality" which accompanied them was to be perpetually excluded from the Church. The Christian *flamen,* therefore, according to this decision was absolutely forbidden to participate in pagan worship under the severest ecclesiastical penalty. The "murder" and "immorality" to which the council referred probably meant the gladiatorial combats and scenic presentations furnished to the people for bestowing the office. A *flamen,* however, who abstained from all sacrifice during his term of office (generally one year), but who at his own expense paid for the gladiatorial combats and theatrical performances was to be readmitted to the Church at the end of his life if he performed the prescribed penance. The last canon that concerned the *flamines* was to the effect that the imperial *flamen* who continued to wear the "crown" but abstained from all idolatrous worship, was to be admitted to the Church after a period of penance lasting two years. The "crown" was the head-gear worn by the *flamen* during his term of officeand which he was permitted to wear when his official duties were over. The above regulations prove that it was only with the greatest difficulty that a man could assume the duties of *flamen* and not be perpetually excluded from the Church. The fact, however, that one who held this office could at times avoid the duty of offering sacrifice shows that the imperial cult in Spain was losing its religious character and becoming a civil function.

A less difficult problem arose in the case of a Christian who might be called upon to fill the office of chief municipal magistrate, that is, to serve as a *duumvir*. During the year that he held this office a *duumvir* was forbidden to attend church. A. Dale and G. Bareille thought that this regulation had been made because the magistrate would have to pass sentence of death and imprisonment, and such punishments were odious to the early Christians. But the reason for the council's action was rather because all Roman civil functions were closely connected with religious worship, and to prevent the danger of scandal to the other members of the community the *duumvir* was requested to stay away from the church during his period of office. This ecclesiastical compromise was made, as Hefele wisely points out, to prevent local enactments unfavorable to the Church.

With the spread of the Church throughout Spain the bishops of Elvira were confronted with the problem whether Christians should be allowed to marry pagans, Jews and heretics. From the wording of the canon which discusses the marriage of a Christian and a pagan, it is evident that in Spain as elsewhere at this time Christianity had spread more rapidly among the women than among the men, for the canon refers to the "abundance of young women" in the Church. The bishops censured the marriage of a Christian woman to a pagan, but attached no ecclesiastical penalty to the prohibition. On the other hand they excluded from the Church for the period of five years those Christian parents who allowed their children to marry heretics or Jews. It was considered that there was greater danger to the faith of the Christian wife and offspring in a marriage with a heretic or Jew than with a pagan, another proof that paganism in Spain was losing its grip on many of its adherents. The bishops, however, threatened Christian parents who allowed their daughter to marry a pagan *flamen* with the penalty of perpetual excommunication from the church. The wife of a *flamen* (called *flaminica*) usually took an active part in the imperial cult, and hence the reason for the council's severity. It is to be noted that the council inflicted this penalty only upon the parents who permitted their daughters to marry a *flamen.*

The Council of Elvira furthermore gave its decision upon three problems that concerned especially the wealthy members of the Church. It was customary in Roman times for the person in charge of heathen games and processions to lend ornaments and dress as stage-properties or for decoration; occasionally he might borrow these things from his acquaintances. As such requests might be addressed to the wealthy Christians, the council declared that anyone who permitted his clothes and ornaments to be used in pagan celebrations or games was to be excommunicated from the Church for a period of three years. Another pagan practice caused embarrassment to the wealthy Christians. In Roman times the pagans were wont to offer part of the produce of the soil to their gods, which offering they regarded as a necessary expense. Hence the pagan "tenant would demand that in the settlement of accounts he should be credited with these legitimate expenses and a corresponding reduction made in his rent." The council forbade a Christian landowner to agree to this arrangement, for such a mode of action would have meant the tacit approval of idolatrous worship. Failure to obey this command entailed a penalty of five years exclusion from the Church. The council also advised the wealthy Christians to have all pagan idols removed from their homes; if, however, their removal might arouse the pagan slaves to violence, the owner might allow these images in his home but was to refrain from doing anything that implied an approval of idolatry. With the same intention of not antagonizing the pagans by the destruction of idols the council prudently decided that a person who was killed in the act of destroying pagan images was not entitled to the honors usually paid to martyrs for the faith.

The dread of doing anything that might encourage idolatry led the bishops at Elvira to enact the famous canon which forbade the use of pictures on the walls of the church. Some Catholic writers give ingenious interpretations of this canon. Bellarmine, for example, thought that only mural paintings were forbidden because there was danger lest the pictures be treated with disrespect when the walls of the church disintegrated. De Rossi asserted that paintings were allowed in the catacombs, but not in places such as Spain, where the churches were exposed to the gaze of the pagans. Other writers thought that the council forbade only those paintings which represented the divinity, not images of Christ and the saints But they read into a canon a meaning which is not there. The bishops forbade "what is worshiped and adored" to be painted on the walls of the churches. Some non-Catholic writers quote this canon as a proof that in the early Church there was an express disapproval of all images, but they exaggerate its meaning. The bishops did not issue any doctrinal statement in regard to images; they merely passed a disciplinary measure, because in the pagan surroundings there was grave danger that the images in the churches would be worshiped and adored. Furthermore, this was only the decision of a provincial, or at most of a national council, that was characterized by rigorism.

The council also visited perpetual excommunication upon anyone who had by magic caused the death of another. The reason for this severity was that the practice of magic included also the practice of idolatry.

Two of the canons of Elvira concern the conduct of Christians at the cemeteries. The bishops forbade women to spend the night there in vigil, because under the pretext of assembling for prayer they secretly committed crimes. The second canon forbade the use of lighted candles during the day at the tombs of the deceased "for the spirits of the saints are not to be disturbed." Very probably, as Hefele suggests, the bishops were referring to the pagan belief that the soul still remained within the tomb, and to the pagan practice of lighting candles before the resting-place of the dead, for such beliefs and practices may have been continued among the converts to Christianity. This canon would seem to have been prompted by some local superstition.

Recent archaeological discoveries offer concrete evidence of abuses very similar to those which gave concern to the bishops of Elvira. Excavations made in a Christian cemetery of the fourth or fifth century at Tarragona reveal several indications of pagan practices followed there. The practice of having funeral banquets there is attested by six tables, semi-circular in shape and with a depression in the center. Two of these tables are covered with red stucco, and red was among the pagans the color of the dead. Near one of the tombs were found fragments of glass, some coins, ashes, and bones, remains presumably of a banquet held there. In two instances tubes were found leading down into the tomb where the body reposed. A vial in one grave contained the remains of milk. A coin was discovered resting on the head of a corpse. This is presumably to be traced to the common pagan practice of placing money with the deceased person so that he might be able to pay Charon for bringing him across the river Acheron. There was one sealed tomb found which contained no body. It was evidently a cenotaph, reflecting the pagan belief that the spirit of a deceased person whose body could not be found required a tomb as a place of abode.

As Père Delehaye points out various practices, pagan in origin, in connection with the burial of the dead were deeply rooted in the customs of the people and lasted on into Christian times. Many of them are plainly connected in their origin with the belief that the soul of the deceased continued to live in or about the tomb. However, frequently they had lost their superstitious meaning and were retained merely by custom.

The Council of Elvira laid down various regulations in regard to the admission of pagans into the Church. The bishops required the catechumens to spend two years in preparation for the sacrament of baptism. *Flamines,* however, because of the dangers to which their sacerdotal duties exposed them, were to wait three years before being admitted to the Church. Actors and charioteers were obliged to give up their professions before the bishops would admit them to membership in the Church. During their period of probation the catechumens had to give concrete evidence of their good faith and sincerity. If they committed sins of adultery or murder, the sacrament of baptism was to be postponed until the hour of death. The council permitted any of the faithful to baptize a catechumen who was at the point of death.

Such then was the legislation at Elvira in regard to paganism and related matters. The bishops realized the difficulties of their flock in a world officially and actually pagan. They were anxious to have Christians live in peace with their neighbors and willing to have them participate in the normal secular activity about them. The pagan members of the communities in which the Christians lived were not to be especially antagonized. Violent and imprudent zeal against the objects of pagan cult was discouraged. A Christian might even allow his slaves to keep pagan images in his home when their removal would give rise to violence and bloodshed. Though a Christian holding public office was exposed to the danger of compromising his faith, the bishops specified conditions under which such office might be held. On the other hand the bishops attempted no compromise with pagan practices or sacrifices. The most rigorous of spiritual penalties was visited on any Christian who paid worship to the gods or directly approved of pagan practices: he was to be cut off perpetually from membership in the Church. Such stern measures were evidently necessary to prevent defection from the faith, for at the time the council was held paganism was the official religion and was closely bound up with many phases of civil and social life.

The fact that so many bishops of Spain were able to meet after the persecution of Diocletian proves that the hierarchy was firmly established in the Romanized southern and eastern sections. The canons in regard to the pagan priests, magistrates and wealthy Christians clearly indicate that Christianity had already penetrated into the upper classes of Spanish society. While the exact number of Christians in the Peninsula at this time is of course impossible to determine, Spain probably possessed one of the largest Christian communities in the western portion of the empire. The epoch-making events that opened the fourth century were to witness the gradual decline of paganism and the predominance of Christianity throughout the greater part of the Peninsula.

Probably in the very year that the bishops of Spain had assembled (306) Constantine was acclaimed emperor by the soldiers of his father, Constantius Chlorus. A few years later (313) the Edict of Toleration was issued in which Christianity was placed on an equal footing with paganism. The property which had been taken from the Christians was now restored to them; they were able to build churches and the clergy received many of the privileges which the pagan priests enjoyed. Though Constantine was not baptized until the end of his life, his legislation was impregnated with the spirit of Christianity. Thus he commanded the observance of the Sunday, forbade the people of the cities to engage in servile work on this day, established episcopal courts, facilitated the holding of Church councils, and used the power of the State to prevent the rise and spread of heresy and schism. "His (Constantine's) vision," says Norman Baynes, "was that of a Roman empire sustained by a Christian God and founded on an orthodox faith."

ATTITUDE OF THE EMPERORS OF THE FOURTH CENTURY TOWARDS PAGANISM

Constantine throughout his life remained faithful to the principle of religious liberty which he had proclaimed in 313. This toleration, however, was not extended to the practice of magic and divination, which was sternly prohibited under penalty of death. One fact moreover in the life of the great emperor indicates the ever-widening gulf between him and the pagan religion. Shortly before his death in 337 the people of Umbria asked Constantine if a temple might be erected in his name. The ruler agreed to their request, but expressly stipulated that no sacrifices were to be offered there. Constantine's refusal to have sacrifices offered in his name dealt a severe blow to the imperial cult which was closely bound up with the worship of the reigning emperor.

Constantius (337-361), his son and successor, did not follow this policy of toleration. In a famous edict of 341 he gave orders that all superstitions should cease and the folly of sacrifices should be abolished. A later edict of this same Arian emperor commanded the closing of all pagan temples, and those found guilty of offering sacrifices were to be put to death. These laws of Constantius were an important factor in arousing the pagans of the empire to action, and in 361 the legions of Gaul unfurled the standard of revolt and acclaimed as emperor Julian, a cousin of Constantius and an apostate from Christianity. On the way to give battle to the usurper Constantius died and for the first time since Licinius the empire was governed by a pagan.

Juliandid not attempt any violent persecution of the Christians and even urged the Arian and Catholic leaders to settle the differences between them, hoping thereby to cause dissension in the ranks of the Christians. He gave orders, however, that the temples of the pagans which the Christians had seized were to be returned to their original owners, and forbade Christian teachers to practice their profession. His efforts were also directed to the reestablishment of paganism in the form of what has been described as a "mosaic of decadent philosophy, bloody sacrifices, rituals old and new, 'spiritualism' and divination of all sorts." But as Julian reigned only two years (361-363) his efforts to revive paganism and weaken Christianity were doomed to failure.

Jovian, the immediate successor of Julian, reigned only eight months, but the mere fact that a Christian became emperor meant that Christianity had definitely triumphed. Valentinian I (364-375), who followed Jovian on the throne, did not antagonize the pagans and proclaimed religious liberty throughout the empire. But like Constantine, Valentinian I refused to tolerate the practice of magic and divination. The civil authorities of the fourth century believed that magic and divination could be used for harmful purposes and that a person might use the information obtained from a magician or diviner to foster rebellion. That their fears were not unfounded is evident from the fact that in 372 a man named Theodore plotted against the life of Valentinian I, because he had been told by a magician that he was to be the next emperor. During the reign of this emperor there were four edicts issued against the practice of magic and divination, and even the study of magic was punishable by death.

A decided change in the imperial policy towards paganism came during the brief reign of Gratian (378-383). Under the influence of St. Ambrose, bishop of Milan, Gratian renounced the title of *Pontifex Maximus,* and had the Altar of Victory removed from the Roman senate despite the opposition of Symmachus and other pagan senators. This same emperor also withdrew from the pagan priests many of the privileges which up to then they had continued to enjoy. But still there was no official proscription of paganism until the year 392, when the emperor Theodosius (379-395), a Spaniard by birth, forbade not only the offering of bloody sacrifices, but also pagan religious rites in honor of the *lar,* the *genius,* or the *penates.* A person found guilty of offering bloody sacrifices was to be put to death, while one who practiced other pagan rites was threatened with the loss of his property. The laws against all forms of paganism were continued by the successors of Theodosius, and the significant fact is that in the last quarter of the fourth century the heathens were no longer designated by the term *"gentiles,"* but by that of *"pagani."* This distinction clearly indicates that paganism was becoming more and more confined to the people of the country districts.

RESULTS OF THE ANTI-PAGAN LEGISLATION IN SPAIN

The effectiveness of this anti-pagan legislation is clearly evidenced in Spain, where only a few pagan inscriptions dating from the fourth century have been found. Two inscriptions made during the reign of Constantine show that many still looked upon him as a god. These two inscriptions, found at Cordova, were dedicated by persons "most devoted to the divinity and majesty" of the emperor. After his death an inscription to Constantine gave him the title of *"divus,"* but probably by this time the word *"divus"* had lost all its pagan significance. Thus Constantius in a law forbidding all pagan sacrifices referred to his father as *"divus Constantinus."* There are three inscriptions to the "divinity and majesty" of Constantius at Tarragona, Cordova and Coimbra. A painting made in the year 388 shows how pagan symbolism and mythology continued to exert an influence upon Christian art. This picture represents the emperor Theodosius seated with the co-emperors, Arcadius and Honorius, on either side of him. In the lower part of the picture is a recumbent female figure partly clad, wearing a crown of leaves and fruit, who represents Ceres, the goddess of fertility. About her are the *genii* or *amores* bearing fruits and flowers. As far as the writer knows there are no pagan inscriptions in Spain that can be traced beyond the year 388.

Only one law in the section of the Theodosian code devoted to paganism refers to Spain by name. In the year 395 the reigning emperors, Arcadius and Honorius, ordered that no one at any time or place might enter a pagan temple to offer sacrifices. The officials throughout the empire were warned that any neglect in the execution of this order would bring upon them the penalty of death. Four years later, however, these same emperors felt it necessary to make an exception for Spain. In a rescript to Macrobius, the *vicarius* of Spain, and Proclianus, the *vicarius of the Five Provinces,* they reminded these officials that the temples and ornaments of the pagans were not to be destroyed, and that any document brought forward in justification of such destruction was to be at once forwarded to them. This prohibition to destroy the pagan memorials of Spain did not proceed from any artistic motive, for in the same year (399), the emperors ordered the pretorian prefect, Euthychianus, to destroy the temples of the pagans where this could be done "*sine turba ac tumultu.*" Probably, therefore, as Geffcken supposes, the emperors had to take into consideration in issuing this order to the officials of Spain and Gaul that there were still many pagans in these regions who would be offended at the destruction of these artistic memorials.

Another law in the Theodosian Code referred to the *Nemesiaci,* a society also mentioned on an undated inscription at Evora in modern Portugal. The emperors, Honorius and Theodosius II, in 409/412, issued an edict which ordered these *Nemesiaci,* and also other members of the societies of the *Vitutiatii, Signiferi, Cantabrarii,* to return to their native cities. Was the society of the *Nemesiaci* a religious society at the time when this edict was issued? St. Paulinus of Nola (354-431) in a letter to a certain Joviusrefers to the cult of Nemesis in such a general way that it is difficult to determine whether or not he is describing an actual cult of the goddess. Commodian, who wrote his *Instructiones* either about 250 or 450, explains in this poem how the *Nemesiaci* were wont to dance about a wooden image of the goddess, pretended that they were prophets, told the fortunes of the spectators, and then proceeded to collect money. Most probably Commodian lived in the third century, and though the *Nemesiaci* may have been devotees of the cult of Nemesis in his time, by the beginning of the fifth century this society presumably had lost its religious significance. The emperors would hardly have tolerated any distinctly pagan society at a time when the practice of paganism was a penal offense, in some cases punishable by death. A further indication of the non-religious character of the *Nemesiaci* is the fact that their name appears only in the part of the Theodosian Code devoted to corporations *(de collegiatis);* had they been members of a religious society, mention would have been made of them in the sixteenth book of the code where pagan practices are expressly prohibited.

The writers of the fourth century give a little clearer picture of the paganism in Spain than do the inscriptions and the Theodosian Code. Thus Macrobius, a pagan author of the late fourth century, may be referring to an actual pagan cult when he speaks in his *Saturnalia* of "the Accitani, a people of Spain, who worship with the greatest devotion an image of Mars adorned with rays, to which they give the name Neton." The Accitani lived, as far as is known, in the northeast section of Baetica. An undated inscription to the god Neton has been found near the city of Merida. J. MacCulloch believes that Neton is derived from the same root as the name of the god of war among the Irish, who was called Net.

During the fourth century Spain was not deeply affected by any of the heretical movements, which in other countries prevented the growth of the Church, and impeded the struggle against paganism. For a brief time, however, in the middle of the century, the Luciferian controversy regarding the readmission to the Church of the bishops who had lapsed into Arianism provoked much bitterness among the Spanish hierarchy. The leader of the Luciferians there, Gregory, bishop of Elvira, is mentioned by name in the *Libellus precum,* which the Luciferians addressed about the year 384 to the emperors Valentinian, Theodosius and Arcadius. This work, in which the Luciferians asked the emperors to protect them from the attacks of their powerful enemies, gives some indication of the pagan survivals in Spain in the second half of the fourth century. Bishop Osius, who has already been mentioned as present at the Council of Elvira, had signed the heretical decrees of the Council of Sirmium in 357. When he returned to Spain, Gregory, bishop of Elvira, claimed that Osius was not entitled to be a bishop in the Catholic Church. The matter could not be settled in the ecclesiastical tribunals, so it was brought before the *vicarius* of Spain, Clementinus. This official, according to the *Libellus precum,* was not a Christian, but a pagan. Later in the same report the writers narrate the persecution which two bishops of the province of Baetica carried on against Vincent, a follower of Gregory of Elvira. These bishops so inflamed the people against this priest (Vincent) that they went to his church, broke down the doors, stole the sacred vessels and ornaments, and "what is horrible to relate, took the altar from the church and placed it before an idol of the temple." These two extracts show that in Spain as elsewhere throughout the empire pagan officials continued to hold high office under the Christian emperors and that all pagan temples and idols in the Peninsula had not yet been destroyed.

The writings of the Spanish poet Prudentius, and Orosius, the friend of St. Augustine and author of the *Adversus paganos,* throw no light upon the state of paganism in Spain in the late fourth and early fifth century. But a letter of Pope Siricius, sent to Bishop Himerius of Tarragona in 385, proves that paganism had not entirely disappeared from northeastern Spain. Bishop Himerius had written to the Pope, requesting his advice on various problems that had arisen in his diocese. The Pope in his reply expressed his joy at the "innumerable people who are seeking baptism." These words are indeed significant, for eastern Tarraconensis had been the center of the imperial cult in Spain. But there was also a dark side to the picture. Many of the Christians had fallen into apostasy and returned to the worship of idols. Siricius forbade these apostates to receive the Body and Blood of the Lord. If, however, they repented of their sins and did penance for the remainder of their life, they were to be received into the Church at the hour of death, for "the Lord does not desire the death of the sinner, but that he be converted and live." Probably these last words of Siricius were meant as a rebuke to the bishops of Elvira, who had laid down the principle that a Christian who had fallen into idolatry should not be readmitted to the Church even at the end of his life.

Pacianus, bishop of Barcelona, in the closing years of the fourth century, indicates in a work entitled *Paraenesis* that some of the people were still practicing paganism. Thus he says that while certain sins can be atoned for by the practice of good works, idolatry, murder and fornication were to be feared "as the breath of the basilisk, as a cup of poison, and as an arrow of death." St. Jerome attributed to Pacianus a work called *Cervus*, which is no longer extant. This book had been written to combat the superstitious practice in vogue among some of the people of clothing themselves in the skins of deers and taking part in immoral rites. St. Caesarius of Arles (470-540) and the Council of Auxerre 573/603 later condemned this same abuse which, according to them, took place on the Kalends of January. The efforts of Pacianus to uproot this pagan survival do not seem to have been successful, for in the *Paraenesis* he exclaims: "What a miserable man I am! What a crime I have committed! I think that they would not now know how to make the deer *(cervulum facere)* if I had not told them about it in my condemnation." The significance of this pagan practice which Pacianus is the first to mention is not quite clear. Perhaps the people by clothing themselves in the skins of the deer were paying honor to an animal totem which their ancestors had worshiped.

The last indications of pagan survivals in Spain during the fourth century are a number of tracts written by a Priscillianist about the year 384. n the first of these tracts the writer expresses his contempt for the pagan gods, and adds that he only read the fables of the pagans for the instruction of his mind. But evidently the episcopal synod (this tract is addressed to the *beatissimi sacerdotes*) suspected the orthodoxy of the writer and demanded a more explicit condemnation of paganism. The writer then proceeds to anathematize all belief in the cult of Jupiter, Mars, Mercury and other pagan deities. In the course of this apology he singles out for special condemnation the practice of some who assert that the sun and moon are gods and consecrate their crops to them in the hope that if anyone had placed a curse on their crops the sun and moon deities would remove it. The bishops would hardly have been so insistent upon the detailed renunciation of all belief in the pagan deities if their cult had entirely disappeared.

FINAL REMARKS

The fourth century, which opened with the persecution of the Christians by Diocletian, ended with Christianity triumphant, at least in the cities of Spain. The extant records of this period indicate that the pagans of Spain did not resist as violently as those of Africa the coming of Christianity.The Church in Spain had not been distracted by the Arian controversy, and the Novatians and Luciferians do not seem to have exerted much influence in the Peninsula during this period.Hence the ecclesiastical authorities were able to concentrate their efforts upon the evangelization of the people. The work of conversion was but a matter of time, for the pagans no longer had any legal right to offer sacrifices, their temples had been closed, and the practice of paganism in any form was a penal offense. But in the closing years of this century there arose in Spain the heresy known as Priscillianism. This heretical movement caused a serious division among the Spanish hierarchy and thereby prevented a full concentration of effort against the survivals of paganism. It also introduced pagan principles and practices. Consequently before discussing the effects produced by the barbarian invasions upon paganism in Spain it will be necessary to devote a special chapter to the origin, teachings, and spread of Priscillianism.

CHAPTER THREE

Priscillianism and Pagan Survivals in Spain

The present chapter is concerned with the history of Priscillianism, which troubled the Church in Spain for almost two hundred years. Priscillian, after whom this heresy was named, is a strange, obscure figure about whom little is known with certainty. The precise character of his doctrine has been the subject of much controversy since the discovery in 1885 of some writings attributed to him. It is necessary to narrate the principal events in his life in order to show the influence he exerted upon the people of Spain even after his death. But in keeping with the subject of this dissertation greater attention will be directed to the effect which Priscillianism had upon paganism in Spain, and the efforts of the civil and ecclesiastical authorities to crush this movement.

LIFE OF PRISCILLIAN

Priscillian was born probably about the year 340. According to Sulpicius Severus, our principal authority on the history of Priscillian, he was of noble birth, enjoyed great wealth, was bold, restless, eloquent, learned, and ready at debate. He was also tireless in keeping vigils, could endure hunger and thirst, had no desire for riches, and was frugal in the use of things. But there was also a dark side to his character. He was vain, unduly proud of his profane learning, and was said to have practiced magic from his youth. Priscillian seems to have come under the influence of a certain Egyptian named Marcus, who was reported to be a follower of Manes. Though but a layman, Priscillian began to preach the doctrine of his master and soon became the leader of the new society. His eloquence and ascetical bearing won over to his cause the bishops Instantius and Salvian, and also a large number of the laity.

The teaching of Priscillian and the secrecy which surrounded the meetings of his followers aroused the suspicions of the ecclesiastical authorities. Hyginus, bishop of Cordova, and Hydatius, bishop of Merida, where the movement was strongest, took action against its spread, but their efforts were unsuccessful. The affair became so critical that probably in the year 378 it was referred to Pope Damasus (366-384). The pope ordered that the teachings should be examined in an episcopal synod, and that no one was to be condemned without a hearing. In obedience to this command ten Spanish bishops and two from Aquitania assembled at Saragossa in the year 380.

The following regulations of this council enable us to form an estimate of the practices associated at this time with the Priscillianist movement. Women were forbidden to associate with men during the time of prayer; no one was allowed to fast on Sunday, nor during the Lenten season and the three weeks preceding the feast of the Epiphany to absent himself from church for the sake of seeking solitude in his home or in the mountains; the Sacred Host was to be consumed in church and not brought to one's home; a person excommunicated by one bishop was not to be received into the church of another bishop; a cleric was forbidden to become a monk on the pretext that the life of the religious was more perfect than that of the secular clergy; no one of his own accord was to assume the title *"doctor"*; finally a woman was not to be admitted to the ranks of the virgins before the age of forty. The bishops rightly condemned these practices, for, if allowed to go unchecked, they would have produced hopeless confusion in the ecclesiastical organization and would have led to doctrinal error.

Neither Priscillian nor any of his followers appeared at Saragossa. But while Sulpicius says that the council condemned Bishops Instantius and Salvian, and the laymen, Priscihian and Helpidius, the Priscillianists in the letter to Pope Damasus stated that none of them had been accused or condemned at Saragossa. The author of the letter to Damasus is undoubtedly more correct than Sulpicius in the present instance. He was in a better position than Sulpicius to know what happened at Saragossa, and moreover would hardly have attempted to deceive the pope, if an actual condemnation of the Priscihianist leaders had taken place. The bishops at Saragossa delegated Ithacius, bishop of Ossonuba (Faro in modern Portugal), to promulgate the condemnation of the practices mentioned in the canons. The choice of this bishop was most unfortunate. According to Sulpicius, he was bold, loquacious, impudent, extravagant, and given to gluttony. Ithacius, and Hydatius, bishop of Merida, were to be the principal enemies of the Priscillianists.

Shortly after the Council of Saragossa some of the Priscillianist leaders went to Merida to effect a reconciliation with Bishop Hydatius of that city. According to their version of what followed, Hydatius not only refused to receive them but even permitted the people to maltreat them. Angered at this conduct, and encouraged by the support of their new members, Symposius, bishop of Astorga, and Hyginus, bishop of Cordova, the Priscillianists decided upon a bold move. Bishops Instantius and Salvian consecrated Priscillian bishop and placed him in charge of the see of Avila in the northeastern section of Lusitania. This ordination violated the canons of the Church regarding the time that should elapse before a candidate might be admitted to further orders. Hydatius seized this opportunity of appealing to Gratian, the reigning emperor of the West, and secured from him a rescript against "pseudo-bishops and Manicheans." Though the imperial order did not mention the Priscillianists by name, they realized that Hydatius would not hesitate to apply it against them. Consequently, Bishops Instantius, Salvian, and Priscillian boldly set out for Rome, determined to win the support of Pope Damasus. But the pope and later St. Ambrose, bishop of Milan, refused to grant them an audience. Dudden censures the pope for not listening to the appeal of Priscillian. Caspar believes that no ecclesiastic, not even the pope, could intervene in a matter that had already been judged by a *lata sententia* of an imperial rescript. It would seem, however, that Villada is correct in interpreting the refusal of Damasus and Ambrose on religious grounds: they considered them as religious disturbers or even heretics. During their stay at Milan, Priscillian and Instantius (Salvian had died at Rome) succeeded in winning the favor of Macedonius, the *magister officiorum* and an enemy of Ambrose. Through the mediation of this official the imperial rescript was revoked and the Priscillianists were restored to their churches in Spain. At the news of the turn events had taken, Hydatius disappeared and Ithacius only escaped arrest by fleeing to Gaul and remaining there in hiding.

This good fortune of Priscillian and his followers was of short duration. In 383 the legions of Britain revolted and acclaimed as emperor Maximus, one of the officers in the army. When the usurper entered Treves in triumph, Ithacius came forth from his hiding-place and requested him to take action against the Priscillianists. Maximus was willing to win the favor of the Catholic hierarchy, and ordered the vicar of Spain and prefect of Gaul to cite the persons suspected of Priscillianism before an episcopal synod at Bordeaux. Instantius was first summoned and after an ecclesiastical trial was declared unworthy of the episcopate. Whether or not Priscillian had determined before the condemnation of Instantius to have his case tried before the civil courts, the fact is that he appealed to the bishops and obtained their permission to be tried by a civil magistrate.

The Pretorian Prefect Evodius, a stern and just man, presided over the trial of Priscillian, which took place at Treves. Bishop Ithacius appeared there, and charged Priscilian with teaching Manichean doctrines and engaging in magical practices. The accusation of magic could be easily made and was difficult to refute. At this trial Priscihlian "was convicted of magic, and did not deny that he had devoted himself to obscene doctrines, and that he had nocturnal meetings with evil women, and was wont to pray while naked." Torture was doubtless used in extracting this confession of magic from Priscillian. The other crimes which the accused did not deny were probably connected in some way with the practice of magic. Thus the word *"obscoenus"* (obscene) was often equal to *"ominosus"* (of evil augury). The meetings with evil women might easily be construed as the magical meetings forbidden by law. Nudity, either partial or entire, was usually required at such gatherings. After the sentence of death was passed by Evodius, Priscillian had to appear for a second trial before the Emperor Maximus. The emperor confirmed the sentence of Evodius and Priscillian and some of his followers were put to death. Others, like Bishop Instantius who were not regarded as serious violators of the law, were merely fined or sent into exile.

Soon after these executions at Treves, Pope Siricius (3 84-398) requested Maximus to forward to him the acts of the trial. In the letter which accompanied the documents Maximus said that the executed persons were Manicheans and were guilty of crimes which he blushed to mention. The principal charge, however, was magic, for at this time the penalty of death was inflicted upon those guilty of magic, but not upon those who were known to be Manicheans. Maximus in this letter to the pope probably emphasized the crime of Manicheism because the law permitted him to seize the property of all such heretics, and Maximus was in need of money.

Priscillian was not condemned to death for heresy, but for the civil crime of magic, and his condemnation cannot be regarded as the prototype of the mediaeval inquisition. The leading churchmen of the time looked with horror upon this trial of an ecclesiastic by a civil court. Sulpicius tells us that St. Martin of Tours, who was in Treves when the trial of Priscillian was going on, pleaded with Maximus not to allow the condemned bishop to be put to death. After the execution of Priscillian, St. Ambrose visited Treves and refused to associate with the bishops who were actually seeking to have the followers of Priscillian put to death. In a letter to Bishop Thuribius of Astorga on Priscillianism Pope Leo I (440-461), however, approved of the salutary effects that had resulted from this trial by the civil ruler. Maximus was therefore justified in saying to St. Martin that the heretics (Priscillian, etc.) were condemned by the secular courts rather than by the persecution of the bishops.

THE DOCTRINES ATTRIBUTED TO PRISCILLIAN

While political motives played a part in the executions at Treves, the question naturally arises whether Priscillian was guilty of the charge of Manicheism brought against him by Bishop Ithacius. Before attempting to answer this question it may be well to summarize the principal tenets of Manicheism. The religion named after Manes was mainly a synthesis of the doctrines of Zoroaster and Christ. It was based upon the essential contradiction between good and evil. Light was the principle of good, Darkness was the principle of evil. All things "spiritual" - the sun, moon, planets, and the soul of man - were good because they proceeded from the principle of light; all things "material" - the world, human flesh, and certain kinds of food - were evil in themselves because they were made by the principle of darkness. There were so many pagan elements in Manicheism that F. Cumont calls it "the last form of idolatry received in the western world." Some of these pagan doctrines of Manicheism are to be found in a more or less modified form in the teaching of

Priscillianism.

St. Jerome refers to Priscillian as the author of "many works" but does not mention their titles or contents. For a long time there were no writings of Priscillian extant except his summary of the doctrines of St. Paul, arranged in the form of canons. But in 1885 eleven tracts written by an anonymous Priscillianist about the year 384 were discovered in the library of Würzburg and published four years later by G. Schepss in the *CSEL*. From the tone of authority with which the writer spoke, and from his description of the journey to Pope Damasus in 382, Schepss unhesitatingly concluded that Priscilian himself was the author. The tracts, therefore, were carefully examined in order to discover the teaching of Priscillian. It was found that when speaking of the Blessed Trinity and the Incarnation the writer used terminology that was open to suspicion. There is noticeable throughout the eleven tracts a constant emphasis upon the opposition between the soul and the body, and a frequent mention of the two classes in the Church, the Elect and those striving to become Elect. Such language, though not clearly unorthodox, might be interpreted in a Manichean sense. The writer, however, condemns absolutely all Manichean doctrines. If these tracts were really written by Priscillian, he did not deserve the severe fate that was meted out to him at Treves. H. Leclercq even declares that Priscillian was perfectly orthodox. It is necessary accordingly to see first whether Priscillian really wrote the tracts and also what his contemporaries or those who lived shortly after him said of his doctrine.

The attribution of these tracts of Würzburg, not to Priscillian but to Bishop Instantius, was first suggested by Dom Morin in 1913. He agreed with Schepss that the eleven tracts were all written by a man who had made the journey to Rome and who had played a prominent part in the Priscillianist movement, but he claimed that Bishop Instantius and not Priscillian was the author. Morin's arguments are in brief as follows: the first and longest of these tracts is addressed to an assembly of bishops (*beatissimi sacerdotes*), and the writer refuted certain specific charges that had been brought against him and the group whom he represented. These charges were a belief in the teachings of Manicheism and the practice of magic. But no such charges were brought against the Priscillianists at the Council of Saragossa in 380, for the writer explicitly excluded this council when he asserted that none of them had been accused at Saragossa. It seems evident, therefore, that these charges were made at the Council of Bordeaux in 384; as Priscillian refused to be tried by the episcopal synod there, he could hardly have been the author of this first tract. Morin also points to the fact that while Priscillian was the popular leader of the movement named after him, yet at this time (384) Instantius was the nominal leader, and this fact may explain why he was the first to be summoned before the bishops at Bordeaux. The second tract is addressed to Pope Damasus and the important part of this letter is the discussion of the legality of Priscillian's ordination to the episcopate. The logical person to justify this ordination was not Priscillian, who was under suspicion, but rather Instantius, who had been one of his consecrators.

If Priscillian is the author of these tracts, it is difficult to explain their heavy and involved style, and also the mediocre defense which he makes of his doctrine, for Sulpicius Severus had praised his literary skill and intellectual ability very highly. On the other hand if Instantius is the author, these difficulties in regard to the style, and doctrine quickly disappear, for Bishop Instantius was probably a man of ordinary ability, who represented a less harmful tendency in the Priscillianist movement, and hence was not executed at Treves, but only sent into exile. To the present writer Morin's reasoning appears conclusive, and hence he believes that the tracts of Würzburg do not enable us to pass final judgment upon the orthodoxy of Priscillian. It will be necessary then to examine the writings of the late fourth and fifth centuries in order to form some idea of the doctrines known under the name of Priscillianism.

Filastrius, bishop of Brescia, wrote his work on the various heresies about the year 383, when the Priscillianist controversy was at its height. In this book he refers to a group of people in Spain, known as the *Abstinentes* who teach and practice the harmful doctrines of the Gnostics and Manicheans. Filastrius goes on to say that these *Abstinentes* - probably the Priscillianists are meant - persuade married people to separate and teach that food is something evil because it has been made by the devil.

Further light is thrown upon the teachings of Priscillianism by a council held at Toledo in the year 400. At this council, attended by nineteen bishops, there was a condemnation not only of the errors of the Priscillianists in regard to the Trinity and the Incarnation, but also of two doctrines of the Priscillianists that are strikingly similar to those of the Manicheans: the existence of a Creator different from the one mentioned in Sacred Scripture, and the belief that the soul of man is a portion of the divine substance.

One of the principal authorities on Priscillianism is Orosius, the friend of St. Augustine. According to St. Braullo, a seventh century writer, Orosius had once been tainted with Priscihlianism. In a letter written about the year 414 to St. Augustine, Orosius explained. the doctrine of the Priscillianists in regard to the origin and opposition between the soul and the body. Priscillian, according to Orosius, was worse than the Manicheans for he sought to defend his heresy by appealing also to the Old Testament (as well as to the New). Priscillian taught that the soul of man came from a sort of warehouse. In the presence of God the soul professed its willingness to fight for Him and was instructed by the adoration of the angels. The soul thence descended through different circles until it was seized by the rulers of evil and, according to the will of the victorious principle, was cast into various bodies upon which a bond was placed.

Priscillian asserted that magic *(mathesis)* prevailed and that Christ loosened this bond by His passion and affixed it to the cross. In proof of this assertion Orosius quoted a fragmentary passage from a letter of Priscillian in which it was stated: "The first wisdom is to understand the nature of the divine virtues in the types of the souls (and to understand) the composition of the body, in which the heavens and earth and all the powers of the world seem to be joined together; to overcome these relations is the duty of the saints. The patriarchs hold the first circle and the divine bond of sending souls into the flesh - a bond fabricated by the consent of the angels and God and all the souls. Those opposite have the work of formal welfare . . ." Here the letter breaks off abruptly, and we have no means of restoring the part that has been lost. Orosius goes on to add that Priscillian taught that the names of the patriarchs were given to the members of the soul, while the signs of the heavens were placed in the body of man, as Aries in the head, Gemini in the arms, etc.

From the words of Orosius and the fragmentary letter of Priscillian we learn that the soul comes forth from a warehouse, professes its allegiance to God, and is fortified by the prayers of the angels. When the soul reaches the first circle, which belongs to the patriarchs, a divine bond "made with the consent of the angels and God and all the souls" is placed upon it. Henceforth the patriarchs rule in the different parts of the soul. Proceeding further on its journey the soul encounters the opposition of the evil spirits and is overcome by them. These evil spirits now cast the soul into a body, "in which the heavens and the earth and all the powers of the world seem to be joined together." Just as the patriarchs rule over the different parts of the soul, so the signs of the heavens, such as Aries, Gemini, rule over the different parts of the body. A bond is placed upon the human body, and it is this bond which Christ by means of magic loosened and nailed to the cross. It is the duty of the saints to recognize this distinction between the soul and the body, and to overcome the body. This fanciful origin of the human soul and body is evidently

56

unorthodox. The opposition between man's soul and body that is here given is very similar to the Manichean dualism.

St. Jerome was probably secretary to Pope Damasus at the time when the three bishops, Salvian, Instantius, and Priscillian arrived in Rome, and presumably became acquainted with their doctrine. He learned to know the Priscillianists better through his friendship with Orosius and from the numerous Spaniards who came to visit him at Bethlehem. In his *De viris inlustribus,* written about 392, Jerome does not pronounce judgment upon Priscillian, but later is outspoken in his condemnation. In a letter written about 415 he calls Priscillian *"pars Manichaei,"* and says that his followers claim to have the secret of perfection and knowledge. He goes on to accuse them of immorality and of associating with women at night; at these meetings (probably the magical meetings referred to at the trial), they chanted the words of Virgil's poem: "Then almighty father Aether descends into the bosom of his fertile spouse in fructifying showers, and great himself, mingling with her great body, nourishes all her offspring."

St. Augustine, who also wrote against the Priscillianists, was in a position to know their doctrines. He was in Rome and Milan, 383-386, was a friend of St. Ambrose and Orosius and corresponded with two Spanish Bishops Ceretius and Consentius. Augustine attributed to Priscillian and his followers the doctrine that the human soul is a part of the divine essence; that on its journey to earth the soul passes through the seven heavens and is cast into the human body by the "prince of evil"; that man is bound to fatal stars; that certain foods are unclean; that marriages are evil and should be broken up. In a letter to Bishop Ceretius he especially condemned the Priscillianists for their immorality saying that the dirt of all the previous heresies had flowed into their doctrine in horrible confusion. The fact that Augustine identified Priscillianism with Manicheism is a valuable proof of their likeness to each other, for he himself had been a Manichean for a number of years.

Finally we may mention the condemnation of Priscillianism by Pope Leo I (440-461), who had been informed of this doctrine by Thuribius, bishop of Astorga. In his letter to Thuribius, in 447, the pope asserts that the doctrines of Priscillian included not only the errors of previous heresies, but also the pagan doctrines of magic and astrology. Later on in this letter Pope Leo mentions that the Priscillianists in the middle of the fifth century taught that the soul of man was a portion of the divine substance, and in punishment for sins committed in heaven had been sent upon earth. The devil, according to them, was the principle of evil, and the human body which he formed in the wotnb of the mother was essentially bad. The Priscillianists also preached the doctrine that the stars exercised a determining influence upon man's conduct, and that the harmful influence of certain stars could be obviated only by the practice of astrology. Hence the pope judged that the Manicheans and Priscillianists differed in name, but were united in the same sacrilegious practices.

The canons of the first council of Toledo and the writings of Filastrius, Orosius, St. Jerome, St. Augustine and Pope Leo I were composed between the years 383 and 447. It is hardly possible that these contemporaneous writers were mistaken in judging Priscillian as unorthodox in many of his teachings. Even if it be admitted that Priscillian accepted the Holy Scriptures, the Sacred Humanity of Christ, and taught that the origin of sin was due to the weakness of the will - doctrines which the Manicheans rejected - still it is diffcult to explain the unorthodox doctrines known under the name of Priscillianism, if Priscillian himself were not in some way to blame. But whatever may be said of Priscillian himself, the important point in the present study is that in the early part of the fifth century the movement bearing his name inculcated many pagan principles. It is now necessary to study the means taken by the civil and ecclesiastical authorities to put an end to this teaching.

THE STRUGGLE AGAINST PRISCILLIANISM IN THE FIFTH CENTURY

Soon after the execution of Priscillian at Treves, Maximus resolved to send soldiers into Spain in order to put down the Priscillianist movement by armed force. He was dissuaded from this hasty step, however, by St. Martin of Tours, who foresaw the evils that would follow. In the year 388 Maximus was defeated in battle by the emperor of the East, Theodosius the Great, and executed at Aquileia. Immediately there was a strong reaction in favor of Priscillianism, though the reason for this is difficult to understand. Popular resentment was aroused against the enemies of Priscillian. Bishop Ithacius of Ossonuba, who had been the principal accuser of Priscillian at Treves, was deposed (probably by an episcopal synod) and Bishop Hydatius of Merida voluntarily resigned his see. Meanwhile the body of Priscillian was carried back to Spain, and there buried amid scenes of the greatest splendor. His followers who had formerly venerated Priscillian as a saint, now began to invoke his name as a martyr. The movement that Priscillian had started passed into Galicia, where it was to become most deeply rooted.

To combat the evils of Priscillianism nineteen bishops of Spain assembled at Toledo in the year 400. Bishop Patruinus of Merida in the address opening the council hit at one of the causes of the recent evils in the Spanish Church, the ordination of laymen to the ranks of the clergy without observing the necessary intervals before admission to sacred orders. It was decided that the decrees of the Council of Nice (325) on this subject should be put in force. After enacting a number of disciplinary measures which concerned the ordination of priests and the penalties to be inflicted upon clerics who violated the vow of chastity, the bishops drew up a profession of faith and twelve anathemas against the Priscillianists. The council next proceeded to examine the Priscillianist bishops of Galicia who had been summoned to Toledo. Of these ten bishops four refused to renounce their allegiance to their executed leader and were consequently deposed. The other six bishops abjured their errors, among them Bishop Symposius, who seems to have become the leader of the Priscillianist movement after 385, and his son, Bishop Dictinius. These six bishops were permitted to retain their sees. Such leniency aroused the opposition of the bishops of Baetica and Carthaginiensis. The matter was submitted to Pope Innocent I (402-417), who upheld the decision of the council and threatened with excommunication the bishops who refused to allow the repentant Priscillianists to retain their sees.

The opening decade of the fifth century also saw the civil authorities taking action against the Priscillianists. In an edict issued at Rome in 407 the emperors, Arcadius, Honorius, and Theodosius II, ordered that the rulers of the various provinces were to treat the members of this society with the greatest rigor. Any negligence in the execution of this edict would entail a heavy fine. The Priscillianists were denied the right of making a contract or of drawing up a will. Their children, if members of the society, could not legally inherit property. An owner who allowed these heretics to meet on his estate was threatened with the seizure of his property; if the meeting had been held without the owner's consent, the agent who connived at it was subject to the penalty of deportation or of labor in the mines. A law issued a year later at Rome declared that Catholics were permitted to seize the churches and property of the Priscillianists. This civil legislation very probably remained ineffective, for in 409 the barbarian invasions of Spain began, and the whole of the Peninsula with the exception of eastern Tarraconensis was removed from the control of the emperors. In 414 Orosius wrote to St. Augustine: "We are more grievously torn asunder by evil teachers than by the most cruel enemies."

About the year 420 St. Augustine was called upon to settle a problem that had arisen in Spain as a result of Priscillianism. Bishop Dictinius before his abjuration of the Priscillianist doctrines at the first council of Toledo had written a book entitled *Libra*. Although this work is no longer extant, yet from the words of St. Augustine, it is clear that Dictinius defended the lawfulness of lying in certain cases, and especially of concealing the Priscillianist doctrines from outsiders. This book continued to be read by the Priscillianists even after Dictinius had ceased to be a member of their society. Some Catholics in Spain thought that it would be legitimate to pretend for a time that they were Priscillianists, hoping thus to learn the secrets of this society in order later on to be in a better position to refute its false doctrines. Augustine refused to countenance this deception which, he said, would only harden the Priscillianists in their habit of lying. He suggested instead that the Catholics could easily learn the secrets of the Priscillianists from those who had renounced its errors, and the surest means of uprooting false doctrines was by instructing the people in the sound doctrines of the Catholic religion.

In spite of the efforts of the civil and the ecclesiastical authorities the evil of Priscillianism continued to grow. In the year 447 Bishop Thuribius of Astorga wrote the letter previously mentioned to Pope Leo I, in which he mentioned the erroneous doctrines of the Priscillianists. In his answer dated July 21st of the same year the pope suggested that a council of the bishops of Spain be convoked and effective action taken against the heretics; if circumstances did not permit the holding of this "general" council, at least the bishops of Galicia should not fail to assemble. As no official record of any such council exists, and as Idacius, the principal source for the history of Spain in the fifth century, did not refer to any meeting of the Spanish bishops in 447, it was thought that the bishops found it impossible to carry out the pope's command. But a careful study of the extant source material makes it reasonably certain that a council was held in Spain shortly after the arrival of the pope's letter to take action against the Priscillianists. The reasons are as follows:

At a council held in Braga in the year 561 Bishop Lucretius of Braga in his opening address referred to a council which the bishops of Spain held in obedience to the command of Pope Leo I. He added that on this occasion the bishops had drawn up a rule of faith which they had forwarded to Bishop Balconius of Braga. Secondly, in the *Hispana* edition of the first council of Toledo there is mention of a rule of faith against all heresies and especially against Priscillianism which was composed by the bishops of Tarraconensis, Carthaginiensis, Lusitania and Baetica in obedience to the command of Pope Leo I and forwarded to Bishop Balconius of Galicia. It is therefore very probable that the Symbol and eighteen anathemas before mentioned, which in the *Hispana* edition are listed under the first council of Toledo were really drawn up at the meeting of the Spanish bishops in 447, Aldama believes that the attribution of the Symbol and anathemas of this council to the first council of Toledo was due to a mistake by the compiler of the *Hispana*. This compiler had before him the Symbol and twelve anathemas of the Council of Toledo in 400, and also the clearer and more precise Symbol and eighteen anathemas of 447. Out of this material he arbitrarily made up his own edition of the first council of Toledo and attributed to it the Symbol and anathemas of the council of 447. Against these positive proofs in favor of a council in 447 the argument drawn from the silence of the chronicler, Idacius, loses all its force. Idacius wrote his chronicle in the last years of his life, when he might easily have forgotten to record this meeting of the Spanish bishops. It is to be noted that while Idacius mentions the letter of Pope Leo to Thuribius, he forgets to add the command of the Pope that a council be held. It seems reasonably certain, therefore, that a council did convene in 447.

The first twelve anathemas of this council in 447 are almost identical with those drawn up at the Council of Toledo in 400. The thirteenth and fourteenth anathemas are directed against the errors of the Priscillianists in regard to the Incarnation and the Blessed Trinity. The following anathemas condemn the Priscillianist belief in magic and astrology, and their false teachings in regard to human marriage- and the eating of meat. The last anathema condemns those who follow the teaching of Priscillian and who seek for salvation "in opposition to the chair of St. Peter."

The results that followed this council of 447 are not known with certainty, but it did not put an end to the Priscillianist movement. The troubled political situation in Spain in the second half of the fifth century, caused by the barbarian invasions, made it impossible for the ecclesiastical authorities to take effective action against the Priscillianists. Moreover the Suevian rulers of Galicia, where the Priscillianist movement was strongest, joined the Arian heresy in 464, and for almost a century were out of sympathy, if not openly antagonistic to the Catholic hierarchy.

THE STRUGGLE AGAINST PRISCILLIANISM DURING THE SIXTH CENTURY

Very little is known about Priscillianism in Spain during the first half of the sixth century. In fact our only sources of information for this period are two letters of Bishop Montanus of Toledo and a letter of Pope Vigilius (538-555) to Bishop Profuturus of Braga. Bishop Montanus lived about the middle of the sixth century. In one of his extant letters to a monk named Thuribius he praised him for his successful efforts in uprooting the detestable and shameful practices of the Priscillianists. In another letter, however, to the clergy of Palencia he censured some of them for holding the name of Priscillian in veneration even though they did not put his doctrines into practice. The letter of Pope Vigilius was written in 539 in answer to some problems which Bishop Profuturus had requested him to solve. One chapter of his letter concerns Priscillianism. The pope condemned the erroneous belief of the Priscillianists that certain foods were evil in themselves and should not be eaten, and ordered that no Priscillianist was to be admitted to the Church until he first renounced this false doctrine and any other errors in which he formerly believed.

The second half of the sixth century marked a definite turn in the struggle of the Spanish Church against Priscillianism. In the year 550 Chararich, the Suevian ruler of Galicia, renounced Arianism and embraced the Catholic faith. The king's example seems to have been followed by many of the people of Galicia, and eleven years later the Catholic hierarchy of this section was in a position to hold a council and take action against Priscillianism.

The presiding prelate at this first council of Braga was Bishop Lucretius of Braga, but the most noted member was St. Martin, at this time bishop of Dumium. The bishops proceeded to draw up a list of the eighteen anathemas against the dogmatic errors and Manichean teachings of the Priscillianists that had already been condemned at the councils in 400 and 447. There do not seem to have been any Priscillianist bishops at this time in Gahicia, but one of the disciplinary measures of the council indicates that some of the clergy were tainted with Priscillianism. The council ordered that a cleric, who did not eat meat, should at least be obliged to taste vegetables cooked with meat in order to free himself from the charge of Priscillianism; if he refused to do so, he was to be regarded as a Priscillianist and cut off from membership in the Church. Most of the other canons of this council were concerned with bringing about uniformity in the ceremonies of the liturgy. As an organized cult Priscillianism disappeared after this first council of Braga.

Even if Priscillian himself were not unorthodox, still it is clear from the testimony brought forward in the preceding pages, that the heresy named after him taught pagan principles, such as the origin of the world from a being intrinsically evil, and the condemnation of the flesh and marriage. Priscillianism also inculcated the practice of astrology, which had disastrous effects in the moral order, for if the stars exercised a decisive influence upon man's life and conduct, the individual was no longer responsible for the sins which he had committed.

Priscillianism survived longest in Galicia, and prevented the ecclesiastical authorities there from giving the people a thorough training in the teachings of Christianity. The result was that pagan survivals were found in Galicia even during the closing years of the sixth century. Once Priscillianism had disappeared the Catholic hierarchy was able to turn its attention against the survivals of paganism. Fortunately from an extant sermon of St. Martin of Braga, we are able to know the kinds of pagan practices that continued in Galicia, and the means which St. Martin recommended to counteract them.

CHAPTER FOUR

Pagan Survivals in Galicia in the Sixth Century

The arrival of the barbarian people in Spain in the early part of the fifth century abruptly changed the political, economic, and cultural life of the Peninsula. The invasions of the barbarians continued intermittently from the beginning of the fifth century up to the establishment of the Visigothic kingdom there. Our information on what occurred in the Peninsula during this period of turmoil is extremely meager. In his chronicle for the year 409 Idacius, bishop of Limica, says very succinctly: "The Alans, the Vandals, and the Sueves entered Spain." Salvian, the stern moralist of Gaul, regarded this invasion as a divine punishment for the immorality of which the Spaniards were guilty. Many of the people of Spain had welcomed the barbarians as a relief from the oppressive taxation of the imperial government, but they doubtless changed their mind at the sight of the ruin and havoc caused by the invaders. Only two years later, in 411, when famine and disease had decimated their ranks, did the barbarians make peace. The whole of Spain with the exception of eastern Tarraconensis was parceled out by lot among the three barbarian peoples. The Sueves and Asdingian Vandals received Galicia, the Alans were given Lusitania and Carthaginiensis, while the Silingian Vandals occupied Baetica. In 416 the Visigoths, who had entered into an agreement with Rome, inflicted a decisive

66

defeat upon the Alans and the remnant of this people made their escape into Vandal territory. Not long afterwards the Visigoths defeated and exterminated the Silirigian Vandals of Baetica. In 418 the Visigoths withdrew from Spain, and were rewarded by the Roman authorities with *Aquitania Secunda* in southeastern France where they established the kingdom of Toulouse. The withdrawal of the Visigoths did not bring peace to the Peninsula. Gunderich, king of Asdingian Vandals, inflicted a series of defeats upon the imperial troops in Spain. After his death in 428, Gaiseric, his brother-in-law, became the ruler of the Vandals, and in the following year led his people into Africa. Thus in the year 430 the Sueves were the only barbarians in the Iberian Peninsula.

RELIGIOUS HISTORY OF THE SUEVES BEFORE 550

The history of the Sueves, the first of the Germanic people to make a permanent settlement in Spain, deserves a careful study. We are rather well informed about pagan survivals in the Galician kingdom of the Sueves in the second half of the sixth century because of the determined efforts to uproot paganism made by St. Martin of Braga. Up to that time we know little about the religious situation there. The Sueves, as far as is known, were pagans when they entered Spain, and thus a new form of paganism, the Germanic, was to trouble the Peninsula. But just how far the pagan beliefs and practices, which Caesar and especially Tacitus had attributed to the Germans, continued to be held and practiced, is a question that cannot be answered with the sources at our disposal. There is no mention of the religion of the Sueves in the extant writings of the first four centuries, nor in the chronicle of Idacius, our principal authority for the history of Spain during the fifth century.

During their early years in Spain the Sueves do not seem to have been openly hostile to the Church. This is evident from the fact that the hierarchy of Galicia was able to take active measures against the Priscillianists. The Catholic bishops and priests were also spreading among the barbarians the knowledge of the Gospel, for in 448 when Rechiar mounted the throne, he had already embraced Catholicism. Whether the ruler's example was followed by his subjects, as was often the case in this early period, is unknown, for Idacius says nothing about a conversion to Catholicism of a large number of the Suevian people of Galicia.

The change in religion did not produce a great change in the conduct of the new ruler. Not long after his accession to the throne, Rechiar resumed the Suevian habit of preying upon the natives of Spain. A number of his people murdered some Romans who were celebrating the feast of Easter at Astorga, and who believed that they were secure from attack during this solemn festival. The Sueves did not hesitate to seize Bishop Idacius, the chronicler above-mentioned, and imprison him for three months. A raid, however, that they made in Tarraconensis had disastrous consequences for them. The Visigoths were at once commissioned to avenge this raid by Avitus, whom they had shortly before acclaimed as emperor. They did this so thoroughly in a battle against the Sueves at Astorga that Idacius believed the Suevian kingdom had come to an end. His judgment proved premature, for a few years later the Sueves were reunited under Reismund. In 464 this ruler concluded an alliance with the Visigoths and obtained as his wife a woman of their nation. Soon after this marriage Ajax, an apostate Catholic, came to Galicia and, aided by Reismund, spread among the Sueves the Arian heresy. As the chronicle of Idacius ends in 468 it is impossible to determine how many of the people became Arians. But Idacius records that the Catholic Church in Galicia suffered very much as a result of the invasions.

The history of the Suevian kingdom from 468 to 550 is veiled in the greatest obscurity. Isidore merely informs us that many of the rulers of Galicia during this period remained Arians. But the Catholic hierarchy continued to exist there, for in 539 Pope Vigilius (538-555), in the letter to Bishop Profuturus of Braga mentioned in the previous chapter, was overjoyed to hear that a number of the Arians of Galicia were seeking admission to the Catholic Church. In the year 550, however, according to Gregory of Tours, there began a series of remarkable events that brought about the conversion of the Suevian ruler and his household and also led to the awakening of Catholic life among the people.

CONVERSION OF THE SUEVES TO CATHOLICISM

In this year the son of Chararich, the ruler of the Sueves, fell desperately ill so that his life was despaired of. Seeing his son in such straits Chararich asked those around him what religion Martin of Tours, the great wonder-worker of Gaul, had professed. He was told that St. Martin believed in the equality of the Son with the Father and the Holy Ghost. The king decided to send legates to the tomb of St. Martin to seek the cure of his son, promising that if it were obtained through Martin's intercession he would embrace the Catholic faith. Envoys were sent to Tours with gifts of gold and silver equal in weight to that of the sick boy. The gifts were offered at the tomb and the legates prayed for the recovery of the king's son. On their return to Galicia they were surprised to learn that the boy had not recovered, since they had seen many miracles wrought at the saint's tomb. The king realized that the fault was his since he had not been sincere in giving up Arianism. He now renounced this heresy, as an earnest of his good-will causing a church to be built in honor of St. Martin, and again sent his legates with greater gifts, saying: "If I should merit to receive relics of this holy man, I will believe whatever the priests preach." On their arrival at Tours the legates would not accept the relics usually offered to pilgrims, but asked permission to suspend a silken cloth over the tomb of the saint. Permission was granted and the envoys placed a mantle above the tomb, saying that if it was heavier the following morning they would accept it as a sign of favor and depart from Tours. Vigil was held that night and the next morning the mantle weighed much more than on the previous evening. Taking up this object, now a precious relic, the legates began the return journey to Galicia. As they were passing through the streets of Tours, evidently with great ceremony, the prisoners of the city heard the voices of the singers and asked the guards what was taking place. The guards answered: "The relics of blessed Martin are being taken to Galicia and therefore they sing in this manner." The prisoners invoked the name of Martin and begged to be released. The terrified guards fled. The bars and locks of the prison were broken and the prisoners ran to the blessed relics and kissed them with tears and gratitude, while the people looked on. The bishop secured the liberation of the prisoners, and the legates rejoicing at this new favor obtained by St. Martin said: "Now we know that the blessed prelate has deigned to show himself gracious to us sinners."

When the embassy arrived at Galicia the king's son, completely cured, hurried to the ship to meet the legates. The king with his household embraced the Catholic religion. The disease of leprosy which was especially prevalent in Galicia at this time was wiped out and those suffering from it were cured. Besides these wonderful events others too long to mention took place. Gregory concludes his narrative with one concise sentence: "The people (of Galicia) now manifested such love for Christ that all would willingly suffer martyrdom if a period of persecution were at hand."

Gregory of Tours is the only source for the events just narrated and hence it is impossible to check his account. Hagiographers, as far as is known, have not pronounced judgment upon Gregory's narrative. In spite of Gregory's known credulity, his account in the present instance seems reliable. He had come to Tours about the year 562, when there were certainly many people alive who had witnessed the coming of the two embassies sent by Charanich to the tomb of St. Martin. Even if there is a perfectly natural explanation for the fact that the silken mantle placed over the grave weighed more in the morning than the evening before, still it seems evident from the church built in Galicia in honor of St. Martin that the saint played an important part in the conversion of the ruler. Gregory would also be conversant with the religious conditions in Galicia from the Suevian legates who passed through Tours on their way to the Frankish courts.

Gregory is also the sole authority for the statement that on the very day that the legates arrived from Tours, a stranger named Martin arrived there. All that is known of the latter's previous life is that he had been born in Pannonia, and had visited the Holy Land where he had become acquainted with the monastic life. Martin's motive in coming to Galicia is not known. Gregory says that Martin was moved to emigrate to this section of Spain by a divine inspiration, and his words are confirmed by the epitaph written by Martin himself.

Shortly after his arrival Martin founded a monastery at Dumium, not far from Braga, which was soon after honored by being chosen as the site of an episcopal see with Martin as its first bishop. His elevation to the episcopate must have taken place soon after his arrival, for at the first council of Braga, in 561, where the bishops signed according to seniority, Martin was third in rank. Besides the monastery at Dumium, he is also said to have established other monastic foundations, but their location is not known. Martin directed the proceedings of the second council of Braga in 572, for sometime between the years 561 and 372 he had been transferred from Dumium to the metropolitan see of Braga.

Martin was not only an able administrator but also a skilled writer. Gregory of Tours says of him that "he was second to none among the learned men of his time." His knowledge of Greek, unusual in the West in the sixth century, is attested by his translation of the *Sayings of the Egyptian Fathers* and of a collection of eastern canons into Latin. For the guidance of the Suevian king Miro, he wrote the *Formula vitae honestae*, and some treatises on the moral virtues. Presumably Martin was the author of the canons of the two councils of Braga in 561 and 572. His knowledge and his position would point to him as the one who would be called upon to draught them, and the canons reveal the use of the *cursus* which characterize his other known writings. He was also the author of many letters full of wise counsels and practical suggestions on the practice of virtue. The most interesting of his works is a sermon, *De correctione rusticorum*, which is directed against pagan practices and affords the principal material for this chapter. Martin died, according to Gregory of Tours, in 580 and was probably buried near the monastery of Dumium.

The manifold activities during his thirty years in Galicia have won for Martin the title, "Apostle of the Sueves." Thus his friend and correspondent, Venantius Fortunatus, in an obscure poetic eulogy compares him to St. Martin of Tours and even to the Apostles. St. Isidore of Seville says of him: "Theodomir (probably the immediate successor of Chararich) with the aid of Martin, bishop of the monastery of Dumium, renowned for his faith and learning, immediately restored the Sueves to the Catholic faith."

EFFORTS OF MARTIN TO UPROOT PAGAN SURVIVALS IN GALICIA

The efforts of Martin to crush paganism in Galicia formed an important part of his pastoral activity. In his address opening the second council of Braga (572) Martin pointed to the fact that unity of faith reigned in Galicia. While the first council of Braga (561) had been concerned mainly with enacting laws against the Priscillianists in Galicia, the second council could turn its attention to the abuses among the faithful themselves. The first canon of this council required the bishops in their annual visitation of the diocese to assemble the people and warn them against the practice of idolatry, and other serious crimes as murder, adultery, and perjury. Moreover the *Capitula* which

Martin translated from the Greek contained a number of canons on idolatry and superstition. As the source of some of these canons on idolatry in the *Capitula* cannot be traced in previous conciliar legislation, it is not at all improbable, as Maasenand Krugeruggest, that they were drawn up by Martin himself. Added confirmation of this fact is that the canons in the *Capitula* on idolatry are in remarkable agreement with the practices censured by the saint in the *De correctione rusticorum.*

The canon of the second council of Braga ordering the bishops to warn the people against the practice of idolatry was undoubtedly the cause of Martin's sermon, *De correctione rusticorum.* This is evident from the opening words of the sermon addressed to Bishop Polemius of Astorga: "I received the letter of your holy charity, in which you asked me to write something on the origin of idols and their abomination . . . for the correction of the peasants." A second proof that the sermon was written after the council is the similarity between the plan of the sermon, as outlined by the council, and that followed in the *De correctione rusticorum.* The canon of the council said that the bishop should warn the people of the dangers of idolatry, murder, and fornication, and emphasize the future resurrection of the dead and the account each one would have to render to God after death. The sermon sent to Polemius follows this general plan. The sermon was probably written about the year 574. Whether it was used by the other bishops of Galicia cannot be ascertained. It is certain, however, that the sermon was known to St. Eligius (590-660), who was active in the struggle against paganism in northern France, for at times he quotes verbatim the pagan practices mentioned by Martin. The abbot, Pirminius, founder of the monastery of Reichenau, in his *Scarapsus* (written probably between the years 710-724) copies the *De correctione rusticorum* concerning pagan practices. Caspari is of the opinion that a homily by an English monk, Aelfric, written in Anglo-Saxon about the year 1000, is borrowed in part from Martin. He bases his reason on the fact that both Martin and Aelfric follow the same general plan in regard to the origin of idolatry. There is also a remarkable agreement between the two writers in their descriptions of the shameful lives led by Jupiter, Juno, Mercury, Venus, and Saturn, whom the people later worshiped as gods. Both writers may have been following a common patristic tradition.

The audience for whom Martin's sermon was intended is quite evidently people living in the country districts. This is clear from the opening words, which are directed to the "peasants." Most of the superstitions were to be found in the country districts, as honoring the mice and moths, and worshiping stones, fountains, and trees. The language, too, is simple and adapted to the intelligence of the country people, for Martin wished "to season the food for peasants with peasant language." The "peasant language" means the simple, popular style, as distinct from the elegant style affected at the time, which Martin sometimes used in his other writings. The racial origin of the country audience cannot be determined, since many of the superstitions which Martin censured were common to the Roman, the Celtic-Iberian, and the Germanic paganism.

The sermon, which consists of eighteen chapters, is made up of two principal parts: the didactic, from chapter two to thirteen, and the exhortatory, from chapter fourteen to eighteen. Martin places the principal emphasis upon the instruction of the people. He believed that the cause of idolatry was not malice, but ignorance. This is seen from his opening words: "We wish to expound to you, my dear brethren, . . . a doctrine which either you have not heard, or if you have heard, have allowed yourselves to forget." Throughout the sermon Martin constantly emphasizes ignorance as the cause of idolatry.

This lack of knowledge among the people should not cause surprise. Galicia had been settled in the early part of its history by the Celts and Iberians, and, as was pointed out in the first chapter, the primitive religions had been deeply rooted there. While Christianity had come to the cities of northwestern Spain in the third century, it probably did not penetrate into the country districts until much later. The first council of Braga lamented the little knowledge of the true faith that existed in Galicia, "the extremity of the world." Besides the Priscillianist errors had taken a deep root in Galicia during the years 388-561, and Arianism had been the state religion there from 464-550. If the first council of Braga had to censure the ignorance of the clergy, it is hardly surprising that far greater ignorance existed among the laity, and consequently superstitious beliefs and practices would grow and continue among this people ignorant of the truths of the Catholic faith.

In keeping with the idea that idolatry was the result of ignorance, the saint did not approve of force being used against those who practiced idolatrous worship. Caesarius on the contrary had said: "Chastise them [people who practice superstition] most severely . . . so that they who are not concerned about the salvation of their soul, may fear the wounds of the body." In the following chapter the harsh measures taken by the Visigothic councils against idolaters will be pointed out. Martin's attitude was similar to St. Isidore's that faith should not be extorted by violence, but inculcated by reason and example.

THE PAGAN PRACTICES MENTIONED IN THE
De Correctione Rusticorum

Before entering into a discussion of the pagan survivals mentioned in Martin's sermon it is necessary to discuss the sources whence he derived his knowledge of paganism. A recent writer, W. Boudriot, claims that the pagan practices mentioned by Martin are but extracts from the sermons of St. Caesarius of Arles (470-542), which were often directed against the survivals of paganism in southeastern France. Boudriot bases his assertion upon the fact that the sermons of Caesarius were known in Spain, and upon the similarity between the pagan practices mentioned by Caesarius and Martin. But despite these facts it is improbable that Martin was a mere copyist. In a dissertation written at Marburg in 1909 R. Boese compiled a list of the pagan practices mentioned by Caesarius, and compared them with the superstitions mentioned in the sermon of Martin. Because Martin censured the pagan practice of honoring mice and moths, which Caesarius did not mention, Boese concluded that Martin did not copy from Caesarius. Boese apparently overlooked some other practices found in the *De correctione rusticorum* of which there is no record in the sermons of Caesarius, and to which attention will be called in the present chapter. In answer to the objection that Martin and Caesarius do not agree in regard to paganism, Boudriot asserts that Martin obtained his information from sermons of Caesarius which are no longer extant. Such reasoning is arbitrary and open to question.

Both Boese and Boudriot have failed to note that Martin's attitude towards paganism is very different from that of Caesarius, and that the two do not always suggest the same means of overcoming the same superstitions. These writers also ignore the fact that the action of the second council of Braga against paganism in Galicia, and the agreement between the pagan practices in the sermon and *Capitula* of Martin are a strong indication that Martin was inveighing against actual abuses. The similarity of the pagan practices in northwestern Spain with those in southeastern France may be merely a coincidence, for oftentimes the same types of paganism flourished in widely-separated localities.

The sermon of Martin opens with an account of the creation of the angels and of men. He first describes the creation and rebellion of the angels, whom God punished by sending them into "the air which is below heaven." The creation of man followed upon the disobedience of the angels. God promised Adam and Eve, our first parents, that if they remained faithful to the command not to eat the forbidden fruit, the human race would be rewarded with the eternal happiness of heaven, which the rebellious angels had forfeited. The devil, envying the glorious destiny that awaited man, appeared to Adam and Eve under the form of a serpent and tempted them to eat the forbidden fruit. Our first parents yielded to the temptation of the devil, and for this sin of disobedience were driven by God from the garden of paradise.

The belief that the devil dwelt in the air was not original with Martin, but had become familiar to the eastern and western world through the writings of Origen and Augustine. The latter also emphasized the fact that God's principal purpose in the creation of the human race was to fill the places in heaven left vacant by the rebellion of the angels.

Martin next proceeds to state that the Deluge, which took place two thousand, two hundred and forty-two years after the creation of man, was caused when the sins of the human race provoked God to anger. It was only after this catastrophe, according to Martin, who here follows the scripture narrative, that men forgot their Creator and adored the creatures of God - the sun, the moon, and the stars. Perceiving this proneness of men to idolatry, the devils appeared to them in various shapes and urged them to worship the gods who presided over the rivers and the summits of the mountains. Later the devils saw men adoring "wicked and abandoned men of the Greek race," such as Jupiter, Saturn, Juno, Mars, Mercury, and Venus. Consequently the demons appropriated to themselves the names of these gods, urging the people to worship them, erect statues to them, and offer them as libations the blood of animals and even of human beings. Besides the deities whom Martin mentioned by name, the gods and goddesses honored in the fountains were also "malignant spirits and wicked demons."

The view that the gods had once been men was quite common

since the days of Euhemerus (about the year 300 B. C.). The doctrine of the human origin of the gods was an effective weapon in the hands of the Christian apologists against the practice of idolatry. From various places in Sacred Scripture where the worship of the gods is called the worship of the demons, the Christian apologists linked up idolatry with the worship of the devil. Martin's whole sermon is impregnated with the belief that the demons are an essential part of all idolatry.

Thus he stresses the fact that the primary purpose of the Incarnation was to free mankind from the worship of the devil: "God seeing that wretched men were so deceived by the devil and his angels that, forgetting their creator they adored the demons in His stead sent His Son . . . to lead them back from the delusion of the devil to the worship of the true God." Before His return to heaven Christ commanded the Apostles to warn the people against the sin of idolatry: "After forty days had passed He commanded His disciples . . . to teach those who had been baptized to refrain from evil works, that is, from idols, etc." In keeping with this same idea he also emphasized the fact that the practice of idolatry is a violation of the pledges which they have made in baptism to renounce the devil and all his works and pomps: "Consider the nature of the covenant which you have made with God in baptism. You promised to renounce the devil and his angels. . . . Behold what a pledge and confession God holds from you. And how can anyone who has renounced the devil and his angels, his worship and his evil works, return again to the worship of the devil?" Martin had no fear of the devil, nor should any true Christian fortified with the sign of the cross fear the evil spirits: "Why does no augury harm me or any other upright Christian? Because when the sign of the cross goes before, the sign of the devil is naught." Finally Martin recalls to his hearers the grim fact that those who practice idolatry will one day be cast with the devil and his angels into the unending fire of hell. Caspari sums up Martin's attitude towards idolatry as follows: "This view of the origin of idolatry through the instigation of the fallen angels dominates . . . the entire sermon, is its governing idea, gives it a constant tenor, and makes it a unified whole."

After Martin had linked up idolatry with the worship of the demons, and thereby made the people aware of its gravity he proceeds to censure the various superstitious beliefs and practices. The first of these idolatrous practices consists in designating the days of the week by the names of the pagan gods, Mars, Mercury, Jupiter, Venus, and Saturn. Martin looks upon these gods as historical personages who lived among the Greeks. He mentions the revolting and immoral lives which each one of them had lived while on earth. Caesarius had cited the sinfulness of the gods as a reason for not calling the days of the week after them. Martin, however, gives a second reason, not mentioned by Caesarius, for abandoning this practice: "Now when almighty God created heaven and earth, He created first the light, which alternated with the darkness seven times during the periods of His labors." After describing what the Creator did from the first to the seventh day Martin continues: "The one period of light, therefore, which was created first among the works of God, was divided into seven parts after the division of God's labors, and was called the week. What madness then for a man baptized in the faith of Christ not to observe the Lord's day, on which Christ rose, and to say that he observes the days of Jupiter, Mercury, Venus, or Saturn who have no day, but were adulterers, sorcerers, and evil doers, and who came to an evil end in their own land." Since a large part of the diocese of Braga belonged to modern Portugal, it is probable that the practice in Portugal of calling the days of the week "*feira*" from the Latin "*feria*" may have been due to this sermon of Martin. Portugal alone of all the Romance lands uses "*feria*" as the day of the week.

Some of the people of Galicia, according to Martin, continued the pagan practice of honoring Jupiter by not working on Thursday, the day set apart to honor this god. Caesarius of Aries also censured this manner of honoring Jupiter on Thursday and suggested that the people abstain from all business and work in the field on Sunday and devote this day to the worship of God. Martin forbade the people to perform any servile work on Sunday. He permitted them on this day to do whatever work was necessary for refreshing the body in preparing food, and in meeting the necessity of a long journey. As a further proof of his kindliness he allowed short journeys on Sunday for a good purpose, such as visiting a shrine or a friend, consoling a sick neighbor or aiding a good cause. L. MacReavy in a recent article claims that Martin's step was revolutionary, and that his explanation of the Sunday repose from labor reduced Sunday to a species of Christian sabbath. However, as Martin's sermon does not seem to have been very well known, his direct influence upon subsequent writers and ecclesiastical councils may not have been very great.

In connection with Mercury, venerated on Wednesday, Martin refers to the practice among some people of casting stones in a heap and offering these to Mercury: "To him, as the god of gain, the avaricious when passing the crossroads cast stones together and offer heaps of stones in token of sacrifice." The images of Mercury (the Grecian Hermes) were often placed at the crossroads to avert the harmful influences which were attributed to these places. Perhaps this practice or some survival of it was still being followed in Galicia, for in this section of Spain the *Lares viales* had been very popular in pagan times.

Besides these gods and goddesses, Martin refers to the Lamias, nymphs, and Dianas who rule over the sea, fountains and forests. The cult of the Dianas seems to have been very widespread. In the life of St. Symphorianus, martyred at Autun during the reign of the emperor Aurelian, the pagan belief in the Dianas of the forests is mentioned. Gregory of Tours tells how a Lombard monk, named Vulfolaic, during his life of asceticism in the forest met some people who had erected a huge statue in honor of Diana. Cabal believes rightly that the name of the popular fairies of

Asturia, the *"xanas"* is derived philologically from the *"Dianae"* to whom Martin refers.

Besides setting apart the days of the week to honor Mars, Mercury, etc., the people of Galicia continued to take part in superstitious rites at the beginning of the year on the kalends of January. Probably the same practice which Pacianus had mentioned as taking place among the people on this occasion, namely masquerading in the skins of animals, was still in vogue in the time of Martin. The saint sought to eradicate this evil custom by showing that the eighth day before the kalends of April (March 25) was the beginning of the year and not the kalends of January: "God made a division between the light and darkness; but every correct division forms equal parts; thus on the eighth day before the kalends of April the day has the same number of hours as the night. And so it is not true that the kalends of January are the beginning of the year." Martin did not recommend as Caesarius did the practice of fasting on the kalends of January to atone for the idolatry practiced on this occasion.

At the beginning of the year some of the peasants of Galicia set apart a day to honor the mice and moths, a pagan practice which Martin condemns and ridicules: "What must we now say with sorrow concerning that most foolish error whereby they keep the days of mice and moths, and if it dare be said, that a Christian should venerate mice and moths instead of God. For if bread or cloth be not protected from them by means of a cask or box, in no way will they forbear to attack things shown to them when they shall find them." This practice of honoring the mice and moths at the beginning of the year is not mentioned elsewhere in ancient literature. It seems similar, however, to the Roman festival of the *Paganalia,* celebrated at the beginning of the year in honor of *Tellus* and *Ceres,* who were asked to preserve the crops from harmful field mice. Field mice in the days of Strabo had brought harm to the crops in Cantabria and also caused a pestilence. Cabal states that owing to the great humidity of Galicia field mice are very numerous and are the plague of the farmer. Caspari believes that Martin misunderstood the purpose of this superstitious practice, and that the people were not venerating the mice and moths but merely seeking to render them harmless. Even in the latter case they would be clearly using some magical means to prevent the mice and moths from doing harm to the crops.

After censuring the people for regarding the kalends of January as the beginning of the year and for venerating the mice and moths at this time, Martin still referring to the pagan practices at the beginning of the year continues: "In vain does man make these prefigurations in order that as in the beginning of the year he rejoices in an abundance of everything, so it may happen to him throughout the whole year." This passage in the sermon is somewhat vague, for Martin does not explain what is prefigured at the beginning of the year. However by referring to a sermon of Caesarius, Martin's words become intelligible. The bishop of Arles censures the people for placing eatables on the table at the beginning of the year. They thought that the demons would eat this food and in return would grant them an abundance of everything during the rest of the year. Very probably Martin was referring to this custom on the Kalends of January when in a later part of the sermon he condemns the people for "adorning the table."

He censures the people of Galicia for observing the Kalends at the beginning of each month, as distinct from the Kalends of January. The Kalends of each month were days sacred to Juno and on them celebrations were usually held in the home. Martin also condemns the people for "keeping the Vulcanalia," a festival celebrated in Roman times on the twenty-third of August. The belief in lucky and unlucky days seems to have been common in Galicia, since Martin inveighs against women who wait until the day of Venus (Friday) for their weddings and who are afraid to set out on a journey on certain days. One of the canons of the *Capitula,* which Martin probably drafted, censures those who practice astrology in order to find out the best days for building a house, planting the crops, and getting married.

From the *De correctione rusticorum* it is evident that the practice of augury and divination was in vogue among the people. Martin refers to those who seek to learn the future by the flight of birds and by means of sneezes. Ascertaining future events by the flight of birds was a popular form of divination among the ancient Romansand Germans. Caesarius of Arles also makes mention in a sermon of these two forms of divination. But, while Caesarius merely condemns such practices as a worship of the devil, Martin shows the absurdity and sinfulness of augury: "Do you not clearly perceive that the demons deceive you in those observances of yours, to which you vainly cling, and that only too often they deceive you in the auguries which you practice? . . . God has not commanded that man should know the future, but rather that, living ever in fear of it, man should hope for direction and assistance in this life from Him."

Another superstitious practice which Martin mentions, "watching the foot," is little known. St. Eligius speaks of the practice some people had of placing an image of the foot at the crossroads, and the saint ordered such images to be burned. The Council of Auxerre (590) forbids the use of images made in the form of a foot. Caspari thinks that the practice referred to is similar to one mentioned in the *Decretals* of Burchard of Worms (written about 1020): "You have done what certain women are wont to do, who observe the footprints . . . of Christians and take away the soil upon which an imprint has been made; they keep a close watch over these footprints, and by means of them hope to deprive the persons of their health or life."- In this case there would be a reference to the common magical belief that an injury could be done to a person by harming something that had come in contact with him. Leite de Vasconcellos supposes that "watching the foot" simply meant seeing with what foot a person entered the room, and drawing a good or evil omen from this action.

Some of the superstitions which Martin censures were connected with the home. One of the canons of the *Capitula* forbids the people to admit magicians into their houses for the purpose of performing a purification ceremony. According to Cabal in some parts of Asturia, before a family moves into a newly-built house, a fowl is slaughtered and the walls are sprinkled with its blood. This may be a survival of the practice which Martin mentions. Martin also disapproves of the practice of placing laurel above the entrance to the home. The use of laurel before the entrance was a custom in vogue among the ancient Romans. They thought that the branch of laurel would prevent all injury to the house and the members of the family, for the entrance was usually regarded as a place most susceptible to harmful influences. Some women of Galicia during their hours of weaving were wont to invoke Minerva, the patroness of weavers. Martin condemns this practice in his sermon, and in his *Capitula* probably refers to this custom of invoking Minerva, when he tells the people not to observe any foolish practice in the making of cloth but to invoke the name of God from Whom they have received this knowledge.

Probably connected with the homes was the pagan practice which, in the manuscript of Toledo, is described as "pouring fruit and wine over a log in the hearth." Caspari, however, prefers the reading "pouring fruit and wine over a log," because there is no reference to the "hearth" in the manuscript of Berne, nor in the homily of Pirminius, where this practice is censured. Caspari finds a justification for his text in the fact that there is no mention of any superstitious practice which speaks of pouring fruit and wine over a log in the hearth, while a passage in a Pseudo-Augustinian sermon speaks of the trunk of a tree as the object of a special cult. However the manuscript of Toledo, which speaks of the "hearth" seems to offer the better reading and is to be retained. It is improbable that the reference to the hearth was added by a later writer, while it is easy to see how a copyist might omit this word.

The passage which Caspari cites from the Pseudo-Augustinian sermon, does not aid his theory, for the sermon merely refers to the fact that the log was honored, not to the *practices* which accompanied this worship. In favor of the manuscript of Toledo is the fact that the hearth in Roman times was regarded as the site of the deity of the home whom the *paterfamilias* propitiated at each meal by casting some food into the fire. Such a custom as Martin describes may very well have been practiced, for, after all, our knowledge of many pagan rites is so limited that the argument from silence has little force.

Among a rustic population many of their superstitious practices would naturally take place out-of-doors, and hence it is not surprising that Martin should mention pagan customs which were observed in the fields, and at the sacred stones, fountains and trees. As an effective means of counteracting the practice of incantations over herbs Martin urges the people to repeat the sacred chant of the Creed and the Our Father, so that, as one of the canons of the *Capitula* mentions, "only God, the Creator and Lord of all, may be honored." In another passage Martin condemns those who mutter incantations over herbs and invoke the names of demons.- It might be added here that one of Martin's *Capitula* threatens excommunication to a cleric who uses incantations or ligatures.

The first chapter of this study showed that the Celts and Iberians regarded certain stones as sacred. As is evident from the *De correctione rusticorum* survivals of this primitive cult still continued in Galicia in the sixth century. In the course of the sermon Martin puts the question: "For what is lighting candles at stones . . . but the worship of the devil?" Lighted candles, according to him, were also placed at the crossroads, and before certain fountains and trees. The burning of candles at these places was evidently a pagan practice, but its precise significance is not obvious.

At the fountains Martin censures the people for casting bread into the water. As far as is known no writer before Martin refers to this practice. Perhaps the placing of bread in the fountain was in some way connected with human fertility, for in Italy, Scotland and Syria women were wont to invoke the fountain-deity for the gift of fertility. Cabal in his study of the ancient religions of Asturia quotes a modern poem, which says that if young women go to a certain fountain and drink its waters, they will soon be married. The people of Galicia in Martin's time may have performed the ceremony he condemns in order to obtain fertility for their crops. Attention has already been called in the first chapter to the cult of *Tongoenabiacus,* who was honored as the god of a fountain outside of Braga. In the inscription written on the stone over this fountain was the representation of a person, probably the god himself, bearing in his arms a basket of fruit. This illustration seems to indicate that this god was thought to give fertility to the fields. It is also possible that the bread was cast into the fountain in order to procure the relief of a sick person, for some of the wells of Galicia, especially those of Guimarens, a little southeast of Braga, were noted for their curative value.

In Galicia in the sixth century certain trees were also the object of a special cult, but the only practice which Martin mentions in connection with them was that of lighting candles. Such sacred trees were thought to be inhabited by benign spirits and were always dear to the people. Thus in the life of St. Martin of Tours we read how the pagans of a certain neighborhood permitted the saint to destroy one of their temples, but forbade him to injure their sacred trees. In Gaul branches of trees were often placed in the water where animals drank in the belief that the beasts would be made fertile. The Germans used the twigs of trees for purposes of divination.

It is here apropos to call attention to another instance of Martin's characteristic mildness. Nowhere in his sermon or in the *Capitula* did he order the trees, stones and fountains - reminders of a bygone paganism - to be destroyed. This tolerance is in striking contrast to that of Caesariusand Eligius, who insisted upon the removal or destruction of these "sacred" places. In the following chapter the stern measures taken by the various councils of Toledo against the places and objects desecrated by pagan rites will be mentioned.

All of the pagan practices which Martin mentions in the *Capitula* are also to be found in his sermon, *De correctione rusticorum,* with one exception. This is the canon prohibiting the people to bring food to the sepulchers and to offer up sacrifices of the dead to God. The words of the canon refer evidently to the banquets held at the sepulchers of the departed, and which in the early Church were known as the *"agape."* This banqueting at the sepulcher had fallen into disfavor with the ecclesiastical authorities in the fourth century because of its similarity to the Roman practice of feasting at the grave and leaving food there in the belief that this was necessary for the sustenance of the departed, and also because of the abuses that occurred on such occasions. Martin very probably prohibited these banquets at the graves because of some pagan practices that marked this ceremony, just as later on in the eighth century the ecclesiastical leaders of Germany felt it necessary to take action against the superstitious burial customs which persisted among some of the Christians of Germany.

The practices which Martin mentioned in his sermon did not include all the pagan survivals, since the enumeration of all these, he says, would take too long. Probably the idolatrous practices that he censures were the more serious or the more common. After describing in vivid language the terrible punishment of idolatry in the world to come where the guilty person would be cast into inextinguishable fire, the saint imagines such a one saying to himself: "Because I have committed such great evils after baptism perhaps God will not forgive me my sins." To this objection Martin answers: "Do not doubt the mercy of God. . . .God awaits the penance of the sinner. True repentance consists in this, that a man no longer do the evil which he has done, but seek pardon for his past sins, and take care for the future not to fall back into them." The sermon concludes with the thought that the speaker has distributed to his hearers the "money of the Lord," which they should so use that each one of them may be able to "render to the Lord with interest when He shall come on the day of judgment."

The *De correctione rusticorum* is not a cold, lifeless tract, but a real sermon. In it Martin traces the origin of superstition and idolatrous practices back to the instigation of the devil, and then proceeds to show the people why they should avoid this sin which is so great an evil in the sight of God and entails such a severe penalty in the world to come. The sermon was admirably adapted to the simple peasants of the country whom Martin had grown to know and love during his apostolate of thirty years. The vivid scenes where he reënacts the baptismal ceremony at which the baptized person solemnly renounced the devil and all idolatrous practices, and where he describes in graphic language the eternal punishment of hell, and his touching description of the mercy of the Lord must have made a powerful impression upon the minds of these simple country people, whose principal fault was not malice, but ignorance. The sermon is a splendid example of the early mediaeval style of preaching.

In 585, a few years after Martin's death, Leovigild, king of the Visigoths, invaded Galicia, drove the Suevian ruler, Audeca, from the throne, and reduced his kingdom to the status of a province. As there is no extant source-material on the history of Galicia in the period immediately following this conquest, it is impossible to determine whether Martin's efforts against the pagan survivals among the people had met with success or failure. While in the following chapter on Visigothic Spain attention will be called to the continued existence of paganism among some of the people in

Galicia, this does not prove that Martin's efforts were unavailing. Years of determined struggle on the part of the ecclesiastical authorities were necessary before these pagan survivals completely disappeared.

CHAPTER FIVE

Pagan Survivals in Visigothic Spain

In the course of the chapters on Priscillianism and on the efforts of Martin of Braga to uproot pagan survivals in Galicia mention was made in passing of the Visigoths, who entered Spain in the early part of the fifth century. Eventually they became the masters of the Peninsula and remained in control until their kingdom was destroyed by the Arabs in 712. The attitude of the Goths towards the survivals of paganism in Spain changed considerably after their conversion to Catholicism in 589. Hence in the present chapter there will be two main divisions, the period from the Visigothic invasion of Spain up to the year 589, and the Catholic period up to the year 712.

The Visigoths, as was mentioned in the previous chapter, had inflicted a crushing defeat upon the Alans in 416. They might easily have conquered the entire Peninsula, if the emperor Honorius had not secured their withdrawal by giving them *Aquitania Secunda*. The Goths established their capital at Toulouse. In 454 at the request of the emperor Avitus, they again invaded Spain and inflicted a decisive defeat upon the Bagaudae and two years later (456) upon the Sueves near Astorga. Under Euric (466-483), the ablest of the Visigothic leaders in the fifth century, the whole of Spain, with the exception of Galicia, came under Gothic control. In 507 the Franks under Clovis defeated the Visigothic forces at the battle of Vouglé, and the youthful ruler, Alaric II, was slain on the field of battle. The Visigoths were thus driven into Spain and of their former possessions in France only Septimania remained.

THE STRUGGLE AGAINST PAGANISM IN THE FIFTH CENTURY

During the fifth century the Catholics of western and southern Spain lived under the rule of men, alien to them in race and religion. The history of this period, as told in the Chronicle of Idacius, which ends in 468, is filled with the description of the raids made by the barbarian Vandals, Sueves and Visigoths. Strongly fortified cities, such as Cartagena, Merida, Seville, Astorga and Palencia were attacked and pillaged by the Germanic invaders. The churches in these places were often destroyed, the people put to death, or reduced to slavery. With the Catholic Church in Spain struggling to maintain its very existence it was impossible for any serious efforts to be made against paganism by the ecclesiastical authorities. Nor did the Visigoths after their defeat of the Sueves in 456 and their gradual conquest of southern and eastern Spain take any active measures against paganism. Their attitude is not difficult to explain.

The Visigoths who entered Spain professed the Arian heresy. This had been spread among them through the noted Cappadocian Ulfilas (311-383) who had been ordained bishop by the Arian leaders at Constantinople about the year 341. But the Visigoths did not become definitely allied with Arianism until the year 376, when Frithigern and a large number of his followers entered the Roman empire and embraced the Arian form of Christianity, which the reigning emperor of the East, Valens, then professed. While Dahn, Uhlhorn and Böhmer exaggerate the part played by political motives in the conversion of Frithigern to

Arianism, it is doubtless true that the Goths were not much concerned with dogmatic beliefs and probably the rank and file of the Goths remained largely pagans. They did not feel the same antagonism towards paganism that the Catholics did. Thus soon after their conversion to Arianism, the Visigoths did not object to the coming among them of Athanarich, a pagan leader who had persecuted the Arians in Cappadocia. During their raids in southeastern Europe and in Italy the Visigoths were joined by groups of Huns and Alans, some of whom were probably pagans. The destruction of churches in Spain during the fifth century can only be accounted for by the fact that many in their ranks were actually pagans or had but a thin veneer of Christianity. It is not surprising then that the Arian Visigoths made no serious efforts during the fifth century to uproot paganism in Spain.

The attitude of the Arian rulers of Toulouse towards their Catholic subjects is little known. From the letters of Sidonius Apollinaris (431-489), bishop of Clermont, and an eyewitness of what he records, it would seem that during the reigns of Theodoric I (420-451) and Theodoric II (453-467) the Catholics were not molested in the practice of their religious beliefs. Sidonius was more offended at the lack of culture among the Goths than at their profession of Arianism. But the toleration which the two Theodorics had shown towards Catholicism was not continued by Euric, who mounted the throne in 468. This ruler, according to a letter of Sidonius, written about 472, sent many of the Catholic bishops of his kingdom into exile so that in many places the churches were without the services of a priest and soon became dilapidated. In this same letter Sidonius thus refers to Euric: "I dread him less as the assailant of our walls than as the subverter of our Christian laws. They say that the mere mention of the name of Catholic so embitters his face and heart that one might take him for the chief priest of the Arian sect rather than as the monarch of his nation." Alaric II, who became ruler in 484, reversed the harsh religious policy of his father and thereby won the loyalty of many of his Catholic subjects.- He permitted the exiled bishops to return to their sees and made no objections to the holding of an ecclesiastical council at Agde in the year 506. But the most signal proof of the young ruler's good will was the promulgation of a new code of laws for his "Roman" subjects. The principal purpose of this law code, known as the *Lex Romana Visigothorum* or the *Breviarium Alarici,* was to modernize the laws of the Theodosian Code and the *Novellae,* which were no longer applicable to conditions in the kingdom of Toulouse. The new code placed the Catholic Church in a very favorable position and also contained a number of important laws in regard to paganism.

THE STRUGGLE AGAINST PAGANISM FROM 506 TO 589

The Visigothic ruler permitted the Catholic Church to retain many of the privileges it had obtained under the emperors. The ecclesiastical courts were not suppressed; in all matters pertaining to religion the opinion of the bishops had first to be obtained; in the code there was embodied the law of Honorius and Arcadius, which declared that the Catholic religion was the "one and true faith." While the laws against heretics, such as the Priscillianists, the Montanists, and especially the Manicheans, continued in force, naturally those that had been issued by the Catholic emperors against the Arians were omitted.

In regard to paganism, the new law code eliminated the numerous enactments of the Christian emperors against pagan temples and sacrifices. Perez Pujol cites this omission as a proof that the Visigoths were tolerant of paganism. But the more probable reason is that these laws were no longer considered necessary. The building and maintenance of temples and their elaborate sacrifices naturally ceased as soon as state support was withdrawn from paganism. Moreover the *Lex Romana Visigothorum* did prohibit paganism by incorporating a law of Theodosius II against "the abominable and deadly sacrifices and superstitious rites which were practiced in hidden solitudes." Those people who were found guilty of offering sacrifices were threatened with the confiscation of their property and the loss of their lives.

While the public practice of paganism had disappeared by the year 506, magic and divination, which were part of the private religion, were still held tenaciously by the "Romans" as well as the Germanic invaders, and against these two types of paganism the code was very severe. In the *Lex Romana Visigothorum* there were not only the laws of Constantine and Constantius against magicians, but also the stern passages from Paulus, according to which magicians were to be cast to the beasts, crucified, or burnt alive. The law forbade not only the use, but even the possession of magical books. Nobles in whose homes such books were found, were to be at once deported, while people of the lower classes were to be beheaded. These laws against magic and divination were territorial and had to be observed by the Arian Visigoths as well as by the Catholics.

The council which with the permission of Alaric II was held at Agde in southeastern France in the year 506, proves that the practice of magic and divination was not confined to the laity, but had even penetrated to the ranks of the clergy. The bishops under the direction of St. Caesarius of Arles threatened clerics guilty of magic with immediate and perpetual expulsion from the Church, and ordered all books on magic to be at once burned. They especially inveighed against the use of the *sortes sanctorum,* which were so called because the books of Sacred Scripture were used as a means of divining the future. As far as can be ascertained, the practice consisted in taking a book of the Old or New Testament, opening it at a certain page, and drawing a good or evil omen from the opening words. The people who practiced this form of divination were known, according to Isidore, as the *sortilegi.* It is evident from these canons of Agde that the decrees of the *Lex Romana Visigothorum* on magic and divination were directed against abuses that actually existed. It is not at all improbable that the same superstitious practices were in vogue in various parts of Spain.

By the new code of Alaric II the practice of paganism became an offense punishable by law throughout the Visigothic kingdom of Spain. But, in order to act effectively against the people who practiced magic, divination, or other forms of paganism, there was need of an active and close co-operation between the civil and ecclesiastical authorities "that those who will not practice virtue by the admonition of the priest, may be kept from doing evil by the power of the king." Various factors, however, made such co-operation impossible during the period from 506 to 589.

There was, first of all, the political instability of the Visigothic monarchy during the sixth century. The Gothic nobles were constantly wrangling among themselves for the supreme power, and they did not scruple at the means used. Thus in 554 Athanagild summoned to his aid the Byzantine troops of the Emperor Justinian in his struggle against the reigning monarch of Spain, Agila. During this period so many of the rulers of the Peninsula were assassinated that Gregory of Tours remarked: "The Goths had adopted this hateful method of getting rid of the kings who displeased them."

Secondly, while there is no record of an actual persecution of the Spanish Catholics by the Arian rulers except for the brief period from 583 to 585 during the reign of Leovigild, there was constant friction between the Catholics and the Arians. Thus Amalaric (507-531) treated his queen, Clotilda, so cruelly because of her Catholic religion that he provoked a war with her brother, the Frankish ruler, Childibert I. Agila (549-5 54) antagonized his Catholic subjects by desecrating the tomb of St. Asisclus at Cordova. The Council of Lerida (524) refused to accept any offerings from a Catholic who allowed his children to be baptized by Arians. The same council forbade Catholics to dine with those people who had been rebaptized. These facts point to at least some proselytism by the Arian clergy. With such open hostility prevailing between the Arians and the Catholics of Spain it was impossible for them to unite in a struggle against the survivals of paganism.

Finally by the time of Leovigild (568-585) the Arian ardor of the Visigoths had declined so that they had become generally indifferent in regard to other religions. Their attitude at this date is well expressed in a discussion which Gregory of Tours had with Aiglan, a Visigothic legate to the Frankish court, on the subject of Catholicism and Arianism. In the course of the debate Gregory said that the disgraceful death of Arius proved the falsity of the religion named after him. To this objection Aiglan retorted: "Speak not evil of law which thou thyself observest not; as for us, though we believe not the things which ye believe, yet we do not speak evil of them, for the holding of this or that belief may not be imputed as a crime. And indeed we have a common saying that no harm is done when one passing between the altars of the Gentiles and the Church of God payeth respect to both." Gregory replied indignantly: "Thou art a defender of the Gentiles, and a champion of heretics, for thou dost defile the dogmas of the Church and dost proclaim the worship of pagan abominations." Animated by such principles the Arian Visigoths in the sixth century could hardly be expected to take any active part in the uprooting of pagan survivals.

During this period (506-589) there was no noteworthy activity by the Spanish clergy against paganism, as far as the extant source-material permits us to judge. It is recorded of Masona, who governed the diocese of Merida about the years 570 to 605, that he succeeded by means of his charitable deeds in converting many pagans to Catholicism. Another Spanish bishop, Montanus of Toledo, in a letter written probably in the year 530, praises a religious named Thuribius as the promoter of divine worship in his province because he had driven out the error of idolatry. These are the only two instances known to us of any success against paganism during the years 506 to 589. In fact this period seems to have witnessed a noticeable decline in the membership of the Catholic Church in Spain. Gregory of Tours, meeting two legates from Spain about the year 583, asked them about the condition of the "few" Catholics who remained there. Five provincial councils were held in some of the important cities of Tarraconensis, and further west at Toledo, during the years 517 to 546, but for more than forty years afterwards the presence of the heretics in Spain rendered any meeting of the Catholic hierarchy impossible. At the third council of Toledo (589), held soon after the conversion of king Recared and a number of the Arian bishops and nobles, the Catholic bishops lamented the breakdown of ecclesiastical discipline. They attributed this laxity to the Arian heretics, who not only permitted the laws of the Church to be violated, but even protected the offenders. The bishops at this council also declared quite emphatically that "throughout almost the whole of Spain and Gaul the sacrilege of idolatry has become deeply rooted." But with the conversion of the Visigothic ruler and nobles to Catholicism in 587, the principal cause of friction between the Visigoths and the natives of Spain disappeared. A new era in the struggle against paganism now began.

THE STRUGGLE AGAINST PAGANISM FROM 589 UP TO THE YEAR 654

In the year 589 King Recared of Spain, a number of Visigothic bishops and nobles and about sixty Catholic bishops assembled at the Visigothic capital of Toledo. At this third council of Toledo the ruler and his followers abjured Arianism and proclaimed their allegiance to the Catholic religion. The council then proceeded to enact laws against the abuses which had crept into the liturgy of the Church during the period of the Arian domination in Spain. One of these abuses was the practice among the people of singing immodest songs, and of taking part in unbecoming dances on the occasion of church festivals. These abuses, especially that of dancing, were regarded as survivals of paganism. The council deputed the bishop and the secular judge in the separate localities to remove this evil, but did not inflict any penalties upon the guilty parties.

A far more serious abuse in Spain at this time was the prevalence of idolatry. The council took stern measures to remedy the evil. In each locality the bishop and judge were authorized to destroy the places desecrated by pagan worship, and to punish those guilty of idolatry in whatever way they could, short of the death penalty. Bishops and judges who were found negligent in combating paganism, and masters who tolerated superstitious practices among the members of their household or on their estates were threatened with the penalty of excommunication.

To merit conciliar action idolatry must have been rather widespread in Spain at this time. But the canon gives no indication of the superstitious practices that survived, nor of the class of people among whom this abuse was specially prevalent. The clause about slaves was doubtless added to prevent any loophole in the general provisions of the canon. It is to be noted that both civil as well as ecclesiastical penalties were inflicted upon those guilty of idolatrous worship, and that the bishop and the secular judge were to cooperate in combating this evil. Such close union between the Church and State was not unusual, and was, in fact, very similar to the harmony that existed between the civil and ecclesiastical authorities in the Roman empire during the fourth century.

A provincial council held at Narbonne in the year 590 gives us an insight into the types of paganism which were being practiced in Septimania, and probably also in parts of Spain. The bishops there censured the practice in vogue among some people of not working on Thursday in honor of Jupiter. Henceforth the council ordered that those who refused to work on this day, except on the occasion of a church festival, were to be excommunicated and to do penance for one year. Slaves were to receive one hundred lashes and their masters were to see to it that they did not repeat this crime. The council recommended the practice, mentioned by Martin of Braga, of abstaining from all rural work on Sunday. It may be noted that the Council of Narbonne ordered a different penalty upon a free-born person and a slave for the same crime. This distinction between the two classes, characteristic of Roman Law, will also be seen in the penalties inflicted by later Spanish councils and by the Visigothic Code of civil law.

The same council of Narbonne also took action against soothsayers and those who harbored them in their homes and consulted them. The soothsayers were to be publicly flogged, even though they were free-born, and afterwards sold into slavery, and the money distributed to the poor. Those who gave them shelter and consulted them whether "Goths, Romans, Syrians, Greeks or Jews" were not only to be excommunicated, but also to pay a fine of six ounces in gold to the *comes civitatis.*

During the half century that followed these two councils of Toledo and Narbonne nothing is known with certainty about paganism in Spain. But from a canon of the fourth council of Toledo (633), which was attended by seventy-three members of the Spanish hierarchy, and presided over by St. Isidore, bishop of Seville, it is evident that paganism had not entirely disappeared. The canon declared that a bishop, priest, deacon or any cleric who consulted a magician or augur was to be deposed and sent to a monastery to do penance there for the remainder of his life. The council regarded this consulting of magicians and augurs as a sacrilege, and the severity of the penalty is evident.

This same council of Toledo ordered that in reparation for the sins committed by the pagans on the Kalends of January a special day at the beginning of the year was to be spent in fasting and abstinence. From the *De ecclesiasticis officiis* of Isidore it is evident that this practice of fasting at the beginning of the year was not peculiar to Spain, but was the general practice throughout the Church.

The fast was usually observed on the second of January. In the office of the Visigothic breviary said on this day, there are many passages from the Sacred Scriptures directed against the worship of idols. One of the *capitula* of this office reminds the people that the idols of the pagans are demons, and warns them against the practice of superstitious rites; the people are urged to admonish and recall to the "path of salvation" those members of the Church who may be guilty of idolatrous worship.

At the fifth council of Toledo (636) the bishops were concerned mainly with preserving the government of the reigning monarch Chintila. Hence they censured all acts of disloyalty. In one of the canons they condemned as "opposed to religion and clearly superstitious" all inquiries into the life of the ruler, and threatened those guilty of this crime with the penalty of excommunication from the Church. The ruler and bishops doubtless felt, as did the emperors of the fourth century, that a person might use the information obtained from a magician or augur to foster rebellion throughout the kingdom.

It may be well to mention here in passing a visit to Spain made by St. Ouen in 641. The first biographer of the saint, who wrote soon after his death in 684, declared that on the occasion of this visit Ouen had performed a striking miracle which won him fame throughout the Visigothic kingdom. A later biographer of the saint, who probably wrote in the ninth century, magnified Ouen's visit to Spain and wrote that on this occasion the saint had succeeded in persuading the pagans of the Peninsula to desert their temples and idols. This second account of what Ouen is reported to have done in Spain is purely legendary.

THE ATTITUDE OF THE CIVIL LAW TOWARDS PAGANISM

Mention was made above of the fact that once the Visigoths had been converted to Catholicism the principal cause of friction between them and the natives of Spain disappeared. Yet for a period of more than sixty years the Goths and the Spaniards were governed by separate laws. King Chindaswinth (642-653) realized the anomaly of this situation and began a codification of Roman and Germanic law that would satisfy the two races in the kingdom. Chindaswinth did not live to see the realization of his plan. It remained for his son, Receswinth, to promulgate in 654 the new law-code that was binding upon all in Spain, irrespective of their race. The *Forum Iudicum,* as the new code was called, is important in our present study, for it enables us to grasp the forms of paganism that existed in Spain in the middle of the seventh century, and the attitude towards them of the civil authorities.

Attention has already been called to the fact that in the Theodosian Code and the *Lex Romana Visigothorum* most of the laws on paganism were concerned with the practice of divination and magic. These two forms of paganism were also condemned by the fourth council of Toledo in 633 and the fifth council in 636. Hence it is not surprising that the legislation on paganism in the Visigothic Code was directed solely against those who practiced augury and magic and those who consulted such persons on these matters.

Two laws against augury were incorporated in the *Forum Iudicum.* The soothsayer and all those who consulted him, if freeborn, were flogged, their property confiscated, and they were reduced to the status of slaves. The same penalties befell their children if they participated in their parents' crime. Slaves who practiced augury were to be tortured and sold into slavery overseas. Another law against augury lectured the people on the impossibility of finding out the truth from soothsayers, for the devil "a liar from the beginning spoke through them." The law went on to state that a judge who consulted soothsayers with the intention of proving something was subject to the same penalties as those who consulted them about the life or death of an individual. It concluded by stating that since augurs were hateful in the sight of God they were to receive as punishment fifty lashes. Though the Visigothic Code was indeed very severe against those who practiced augury, it did not inflict upon them the death penalty, as did the Theodosian Code.

Besides condemning the practice of augury, the *Forum Iudicum* also contained some stern laws against magic, especially that intended to injure the person or property of another. Under this heading of "harmful" magic, poisoning was included. The idea, prevalent among the Romans and Germans, that poisoning was in some way connected with magic still persisted among the legislators of Spain in the middle of the seventh century. The same section of the code which treats of magicians also treats of poisoners. They believed, for example, that certain women who committed the crime of adultery could by some magical potion so change and derange the minds of their husbands that the latter were unable to accuse them of adultery in the public courts, or even to depart from them. In such a case the law provided that the children of the couple, if of legal age, could give testimony in court against the adulteress; if, however, they were not old enough, the relatives of the husband were to conduct the accusation. Another law stated that a person who gave a potion to a pregnant woman for the purpose of causing an abortion was to suffer the penalty of death. A slave who tried to secure this potion in order to commit an abortion was to receive two hundred lashes, while a free-born person, guilty of this same crime, was to lose the dignity of her rank, and to be sent as a slave to whosoever should be named by the king. Finally, the law stated that anyone, whether slave or free, who caused the death of another by poisoning, should himself be put to death. If, however, his attempts at poisoning proved unsuccessful, the poisoner was to become the slave of his intended victim.

Besides the civil penalties which the *Forum Iudicum* inflicted for these offences there doubtless were canonical prohibitions. Thus in the council of Lerida (524) it was decreed that a person who gave poison to another for the sake of committing an abortion was to be excluded from Communion for life. Perhaps the same ecclesiastical penalty was attached to this crime in the Catholic period of Visigothic Spain.

The *Forum Iudicum* sternly punished the use of magic to injure the person or property of another. One of these laws was directed against enchanters and invokers of tempests, who by incantations were said to bring down storms upon the vineyards and crops of others, and who invoked the devil and thereby disturbed men's minds. These words were taken almost verbatim from an interpretation of a law in the *Lex Romana Visigothorum,* issued by the emperor Constantine in 318. While Roman law left the penalty indeterminate, the Visigothic Code ordered that these magicians should receive two hundred lashes and the punishment of *decalvatio.* The guilty one was to be led about the ten neighboring estates in order that the sight of this punishment might deter others from committing this crime. This regulation was similar to, but not as harsh as a law found in the Capitulary of Chur (800/820). This same Visigothic law ordered that a person found guilty of magic was either to be cast into prison or brought before the king, who could do with him as he pleased. Those who consulted a magician were to receive as punishment two hundred lashes.

Another law of this code stated that a magician who placed ligatures or other charms upon persons or upon their beasts with the intention of killing or harming them, or who sought by magical charms to injure the property of another, was to be punished in the same way as he had intended to injure the person or property of his victim.

An interesting law on magic was concerned with robbing a coffin for some magical purpose. This is the only mention of such magic among the Visigoths; the only other law concerned with robbing a grave was directed against those who committed this crime for the sake of enriching themselves. Those who robbed a coffin for a magical purpose were fined twelve *solidi,* which were to be given to the heirs of the deceased. There is here very probably a reference to necromancy, which Isidore defines as uttering incantations over a corpse in the belief that the dead person would arise, and utter words of prophecy or give answer to questions put to it. Isidore goes on to add that since the demons [always associated with idolatry and magic] love blood, the necromancer in performing his magical rites always used blood mixed with water. Among the Greeks and Romans the evocation of the dead took place in caverns and near rivers and lakes where communication with the abodes of the dead was thought to be easier.

The strict punishment meted out to those guilty of magic shows quite clearly the horror that the law-makers of Spain felt towards this crime. Still they did not wish to see injustice done. This is evident from a decision of the council of Merida (666) which was held shortly after the promulgation of the *Forum Iudicum.* The complaint was made to the bishops at this council that certain priests in time of sickness believed that their illness had been caused by some magical rites which the members of their household had practiced, and ordered the suspected persons to be tortured. The council in answer to this complaint declared that in future a priest who should suspect anyone of doing injury to him by the practice of magic was to bring the matter before the bishop of the diocese. The latter was to delegate certain worthy laymen as judges. If the accused person was found guilty of the charge of magic the judges were to inform the bishop, who was to inflict a penalty upon the criminal severe enough to deter others from committing this crime. A priest who did not follow this procedure when he suspected some one of magic was threatened with the penalty of deposition and excommunication.

PAGAN SURVIVALS FROM 654 TO 711

The laws against augury and magic were the only pagan survivals with which the *Forum Iudicum* was concerned. There is no indication in the law code that any other superstitious practices were in vogue among the people in the middle of the seventh century. But suddenly in the closing years of the Visigothic kingdom other forms of paganism - worshiping fountains, trees and stones - became serious enough to deserve special legislation at the national councils of Toledo in 681 and in 693. During the century that elapsed between the third council of Toledo in 589 and the twelfth in 681 it is difficult to believe that, if these pagan practices were regarded as a menace, zealous and influential bishops such as Isidore, Ildefonse, Braulio and Fructuosus would not have taken counsel on this evil and suggested means to remove it. Besides, if the superstitious rites at the fountains, trees and stones were very prevalent they would doubtless have been severely censured and forbidden in the law code issued by Receswinth in 654. It is quite evident from the canons of the last councils of Toledo that the long reign of Receswinth (653-672) witnessed a marked deterioration in the ecclesiastical organization and this decline brought about *indirectly* the revival of paganism.

The reign of Receswinth had begun very auspiciously. Immediately upon the death of his father, Chindaswinth, in 653, he had convoked a council at Toledo and requested the bishops to dispense him from the oath which he and his father had taken to punish all political offenders. One of the favorite counselors in the early part of his reign was St. Fructuosus, the metropolitan of Braga, and the founder of numerous monasteries in Galicia. But Receswinth, although well-intentioned, was very dissolute. During the remaining sixteen years of his reign no councils were held at

Toledo, a fact which the bishops deplored at the eleventh council held after his death in 675. The opening words of the eleventh council declared that the long period of years during which the light of the councils had been withdrawn, had led to an increase of vice and ignorance "the mother of all errors." Later on they attributed the lack of discipline in the Church to the fact that no one could correct the erring, since the word of God was sent into exile. St. Ildefonse, who governed the see of Toledo during the greater part of Receswinth's reign, referred in a veiled manner to the fact that the Church in Spain had fallen upon evil days. In a letter to Bishop Quiricus of Barcelona he wrote: "I should say more, if the pressure of woes permitted." In another letter to the same bishop he added: "The necessity of the times so wears down the spirit that there is no joy in life because of the evils that threaten."

The sad condition of the Church in Spain in 675 is reflected in the canons of the eleventh council of Toledo. The bishops at this council were concerned not so much with the vices of the laity as with those that had crept in among the clergy. They censured the members of the hierarchy who did not insist upon the priests of their dioceses preaching the word of God and instructing the people. They threatened with the penalty of excommunication the members of the clergy who scandalized the faithful by living at discord with one another. The council declared that any bishop who disgraced his calling by his immoral conduct or who caused others to be murdered or injured was to be deposed and imprisoned for life. The same penalties befell a bishop who in his capacity as judge passed sentence of death, or ordered a person on trial to be subjected to physical punishment. The council forbade the practice of simony, which was prevalent among the clergy, and even deemed it necessary to require of all candidates for sacred orders a special promise that they would conscientiously fulfill the duties of their sacred calling. The council praised Wamba (672-680), who had succeeded Receswinth upon the throne, as "the restorer of ecclesiastical discipline in our time." Though the eleventh council concerned itself in the main with the vices of the clergy it is not difficult to believe that the moral condition of the laity was far worse, and that in such a soil pagan practices which had probably never died out among some of the people would again spring into life. This is exactly the condition of affairs that confronted the twelfth council of Toledo in 681.

Erwig (680-693) who had become ruler of Spain in 680 under circumstances that have left a stain upon his memory, at once proceeded to call a meeting of the Spanish hierarchy at Toledo. It was attended by thirty-five prelates from all parts of Spain. The ruler urged the assembled bishops to take immediate action against the abuses that had arisen in the kingdom in order that "by your zealous government the earth may be purged of the contagion of wickedness." One of the principal evils that engaged the attention of the bishops was that of idolatry.

The eleventh canon of this council begins with the words of Exodus against the worship of idols: "Thou shalt not make to thyself a graven thing, etc.," and quoted the stern penalty of Deuteronomy against idolaters: "Thou shalt bring forth the man or woman who have committed that most wicked thing [idolatry] and they shall be stoned." The council warned all who practiced superstitious worship that they were offering sacrifices to the devil. It ordered that all the places desecrated by pagan worship should be destroyed. Slaves guilty of idolatrous practices were to be lashed and brought in chains before their masters, who had to promise under oath not to allow them to practice such idolatry in future. If the master was unwilling to keep the erring slaves the judge was to bring them before the king, who might dispose of the slaves as he willed. A master who did not punish this crime of idolatry not only incurred the penalty of excommunication but also lost all legal claims to the services of the slaves. Free-born persons, guilty of idolatrous worship, were to be excommunicated and kept in close confinement.

It is evident from this canon that the cult of the fountains, stones and trees, which was practiced by the natives of Spain before the coming of Christianity, and which St. Martin of Braga censured in the *De correctione rusticorum,* was still in vogue in the year 681. The fact that the greater part of this canon is concerned with slaves indicates that idolatry was especially prevalent among the lower classes of Spanish society. The same policy which the third council of Toledo in 589 had recommended was still being followed by the twelfth council in 681. The bishop and the secular judge were charged with the destruction of the "sacred" fountains, stones, and trees, and the prosecution of idolaters. Two penalties were inflicted by the twelfth council of Toledo upon those who practiced or connived at idolatry, which were not mentioned at the third council of Toledo: First, a free-born person, guilty of idolatrous worship, was to be kept in close confinement; secondly, a master who did not punish the members of his household for taking part in pagan practices was threatened with the loss of their services. Since at this twelfth council of Toledo there were present bishops from all parts of Spain it is impossible to judge from the wording of the canon where idolatry was especially practiced. But the writings of a contemporary, St. Valerius, indicate with certainty one of these localities.

Valerius *(c.* 630-695) before his appointment as abbot of the monastery of San Pedro de Montes, founded by St. Fructuosus, had lived for many years as a hermit in the solitary regions of Galicia. An account of his experiences during these years, written by himself, has come down to us. In this autobiography Valerius describes the sad condition of the monastic life in Galicia, where people from the lowest classes of society were admitted to the cloister and some were even forced to become monks in order that the monasteries might not remain empty. Instead of practicing virtue these monks associated with people who had committed robbery, murder, and who practiced magic and other unspeakable crimes. In this autobiography Valerius tells us how he chanced upon a nocturnal meeting in the forest and gives a vivid picture of the unbecoming songs and dances in which a priest, forgetful of his sacred calling, played the principal part. Valerius also describes a meeting he had with some peasants who were practising idolatrous worship on the top of a mountain. As Valerius says that he was then in the mountains not far from Astorga, perhaps the cult he saw was a survival of the worship of Jupiter *Candamius,* who was honored on a mountain of this region, known today as Candanedo. At the sight of these abominable practices Valerius was filled with anger. He at once summoned a number of faithful Christians and proceeded to rout these worshipers and destroy their sanctuaries. Whether the people who practiced these pagan sacrifices were actually Christians or not is difficult to determine. The fact that Valerius summoned "faithful Christians" would seem to imply that these peasants, like those in the time of Martin of Braga, were indeed Christians who had fallen into gross errors.

The thirteenth council of Toledo (683) says nothing about paganism among the people. One canon of this council proves, however, that some of the priests were guilty of superstitious practices. These unworthy clerics who nourished a grievance against others were wont to put on garments of mourning, to close the doors of the church, to strip the altar of its ornaments, and to suspend divine services. Gratian quoted this canon and placed this abuse under the title of magic. Perhaps these priests felt that they could force God, as it were, to punish their enemies by their refusal to hold services in His honor, The council ordered that priests guilty of these abuses were to be deposed and sentenced to perpetual disgrace.

There is no mention of paganism at the fourteenth and fifteenth councils of Toledo, but at the sixteenth council (693) the question of pagan practices was again discussed. In the *tomus* which Egica (688-702) addressed to the assembled prelates he declared that the many misfortunes from which the land suffered were a punishment from God for the sins of the people. One of these evils was the prevalence of pagan practices. The ruler suggested that the things offered to idols by peasants or others should be taken to the nearest church and exposed there in the sight of the superstitious people who had made these offerings. He also urged that a bishop or judge who was found negligent in combating superstition and idolatry should be deposed from office for a year and that a more zealous ecclesiastic or official should be chosen. The bishops proceeded to enact the laws which Egica had thought advisable. They merely added that a person of noble rank who hindered a bishop or judge in the prosecution of idolatry was to be fined three pounds of gold; a person of lower rank guilty of this same crime was to receive one hundred lashes, to suffer the penalty of *decalvatio,* and to have half of his property confiscated by the state.

The regulation of this council indicates that the places defiled by pagan practices were not yet destroyed and that many people were still practicing idolatry. The persistence of these pagan practices was due perhaps to the indifference of the bishops and judges in the performance of their duties, and hence the new enactment of this council that more zealous bishops and judges should be chosen. The council also added new penalties when it declared that people who hindered the prosecution of idolatry, if of noble birth, were to be fined, if not of noble birth, were to be subjected to bodily punishment and threatened with the loss of half of their property.

But the most striking departure from previous conciliar legislation on paganism in Spain was the order of Egica that things offered to idols were to be placed in the churches. The objects meant were probably the ex-votos and vases which the superstitious people placed at their sacred fountains, stones and trees. The idea for this regulation may have come from the letter of St. Augustine to Publicola, wherein he stated: "When temples, idols, etc., are placed at the service of God, the same thing happens to them as when impious and sinful men are converted to the true faith."

The Spanish king and bishops had probably heard of the policy that Pope Gregory the Great had recommended to the abbot Mellitus in the conversion of the pagan Anglo-Saxons to Christianity. According to Gregory the temples of the pagans were to be sprinkled with holy water; altars and relics were to be placed in them, and thus the worship paid to demons would be transferred to the one true God. In the blessing of vases in the Mozarabic rite the priest asked God to purify them from all uncleanness. Perhaps, as Dom Férotin suggests, this was because these vases had formerly been used in the worship of pagan idols.

At the seventeenth council of Toledo (694) no special legislation was enacted in regard to pagan survivals. The bishops, however, censured the conduct of certain priests who celebrated a Requiem Mass for a living person with the intention of procuring the death of this individual. This canon is a sad reflection upon the state of the Spanish Church at this period when some of its anointed ministers used the most sacred rite of their religion as a form of magic to wreak vengeance upon their enemies. The council ordered that such priests were to be deposed; both they and the individuals who requested them to celebrate this Requiem Mass were to be sent into perpetual exile, and only in their last moments were they permitted to receive Holy Communion.

Under this same ruler Egica or perhaps his son Witiza (701-711) the ordeal by hot water was legalized. This is the only instance of the ordeal in Visigothic Spain, and strangely enough was probably the last law issued by a Visigothic ruler. Mention of the ordeal is included in the present study because, according to the more commonly accepted opinion today, the ordeal was a survival of Germanic paganism. The reason for the ordeal is stated in the law itself. Many free-born persons had complained of the fact that they had been subjected to torture in law suits involving a sum of money of less than three hundred *solidi,* in which cases the law forbade freeborn persons to be tortured. The king, therefore, decided that in cases where the sum of money in question was less than three hundred *solidi,* the accused person was to be subjected to the ordeal by hot water. If this ordeal proved him guilty, then torture was to be used; if; however, the ordeal proved the innocence of the accused person he was not to be subjected to torture. The same procedure (ordeal and torture) was to be followed in the case of a person whose testimony was regarded with suspicion. There is no mention of a religious ceremony on the occasion of this ordeal.

F. Dahn claims that the ordeal was introduced into Visigothic law because of the Franks, who had settled in Spain. This opinion has been rejected by most writers. J. Ficker asserts with greater probability that the ordeals bad never died out among the lower classes of the population, who had been little affected by the law code of Receswinth, and that their practices came to the surface and were legalized in the closing years of the Visigothic monarchy. The writer believes that the process mentioned by Ficker was hastened by the fact that King Wamba had deprived many people in Spain of the right of giving testimony in court, because they had riot assisted him in crushing the rebellion of Paul, a Visigothic noble, in 673. Unable to settle their disputes legally these people might easily revert to the old Germanic custom of the ordeal. Moreover the last quarter of the seventh century witnessed not only a marked decline in ecclesiastical discipline but also the menacing growth of perjury. The bishops at the sixteenth council of Toledo lamented the fact that "the sin of perjury has become deeply rooted." The following council declared that one of the intentions for which the litanies should be said was to make reparation for the sins of perjury. As the Frankish rulers at a later date legalized the use of the ordeal to prevent the sin of perjury, so perhaps Egica or Witiza hoped by means of the ordeal to deter people from giving perjured testimony in court.

THE INDIRECT MEANS USED IN THE STRUGGLE AGAINST PAGANISM

Besides the action taken by the Church councils and the civil authorities of Visigothic Spain to counteract the survivals of paganism among the people attention must also be drawn to the indirect means used in this struggle.

As St. Martin of Braga had pointed out in his sermon *De correctione rusticorum,* the worship of the pagan gods and the survivals of paganism were due principally to the ignorance of the people. To offset the harmful effects of ignorance there was during the seventh century in Spain an insistence upon the education of the clergy, the leaders of the people. In fostering clerical education in Visigothic Spain the name of St. Isidore of Seville (560-636) is outstanding. Isidore, the counselor of kings, and the leading ecclesiastic of his time, seemed to realize more clearly than any of his countrymen the need of education, if the people of Spain were to become Christians in fact as well as in name. The primary motive of his literary activity was, according to his friend, St. Braulio: "to restore the monuments of the ancients lest our crudeness become altogether inveterate." Among the ancients Isidore included the early Christian as well as the pagan writers. He did not approve, however, of the pagan classics simply because of the esthetic benefit that was to be derived from perusing them. In his rule for monks, he forbade the members of the monastery to read the works of the pagan authors "for it is better to be ignorant of their pernicious teachings than by reading them to fall into the snare of error." In the chapter of the *Sententiae* devoted to a discussion of the pagan writings, he begins with a condemnation of the pagan poets: "Sacrifice is offered to the demons not only by placing incense before them but also by listening with pleasure to the words of the pagan poets." He then goes on to praise the simple style of the Sacred Scriptures in contrast to the florid and ornate language of the pagan writers. He counsels his readers to avoid the pagan writings out of love for the Sacred Scriptures. But he concludes this discussion by stating: "it is better to be grammarians than heretics . . . for the art of the grammarians can lead to [eternal] life, when it is elevated to better uses." In many of his other writings, such as the *Etymologiae, De natura rerum,* and the *Differentiae* he borrows citations from the pagan writers.

It is evident from what has just been said that Isidore was not consistent in his attitude toward the writings of the pagans. On the one hand he saw the dangers which the pagan classics had for the Christians. His harshness towards the pagan poets is easily accounted for when it is remembered that he regards them as the "theologians" of paganism. On the other hand Isidore realized that the clerics would have difficulty in obtaining any education at all, if the reading of the pagan books were entirely forbidden, and hence ignorance would be the result. In his opinion ignorance was far more dangerous to the faith and morals of the Christians than an acquaintance with the pagan writings. "Ignorance," he said, "is the mother of all errors, and the nurse of vices." And again "the ignorant man is easily deceived." Consequently Isidore permitted the reading of the pagan writers merely to avoid the greater evil of ignorance. He never felt the same enthusiasm for the pagan classics as did Cassiodorus. Perhaps he deemed the brief extracts from the pagan authors which are found in his writings sufficient, so that people might not have to delve too deeply into the original works and thus endanger the salvation of their souls.

The education which Isidore had in view was principally that of the clergy. His writings on the scriptures, dogmatic and moral theology probably served the same purpose as the textbooks on these subjects that are used in Catholic seminaries today. But aside from these sacred sciences Isidore was also interested in purely secular subjects. In the preface to the *De natura rerum,* which is concerned with the natural sciences, he wrote: "To know the nature of these things is not superstitious knowledge if studied in the light of sane and sober doctrine." It is not difficult to realize the efficacy of a work such as this in counteracting the survivals of paganism. He explained, for example, the cause of rain in a natural and scientific manner. This information showed the absurdity of the belief that "storm-makers" *(tempestarii)* could by some magical process produce rain. Isidore dedicated this book, *De natura rerum,* to King Sisebut of Spain (612-620). The ruler replied with a poem to Isidore in which he described the manner in which an eclipse of the moon took place. But before describing this phenomenon Sisebut first rejected the superstitious explanation which the people gave for the eclipse. They thought, he said, that as the caves grew dark, the moon was being drawn beneath the shades of the lower world by the wailing of the "dreadful woman" and when "its high-wandering mirror was veiled" it passed like a mortal into the waters of the river Styx. Hence on such occasions they were wont to make a loud noise with some instruments in the belief that this clamor would save the moon from destruction. Sisebut then proceeded to give in verse the same scientific explanation of the lunar eclipse that Isidore had given in his *De natura rerum.* Doubtless the writings of the bishop and ruler aided indirectly in curbing the foolish practices which the people performed when an eclipse took place.

Isidore's best-known work, the *Etymologiae,* was of great value in the education of the people. It was one of a series of works on Latin educational tradition beginning with Cato, the purpose of which was to summarize information primarily in the field of the liberal arts, but on other subjects as well. Hence it served as a convenient manual of information on various topics, for in Spain at this time the works of earlier writers were hardly accessible to most of the clergy. However, Isidore reflects in many places the decline in scientific thought which began after the Hellenistic age. Thus he regards comets as harbingers of coming calamities, a common belief in the Middle Ages, which arose probably from the fact that a comet had appeared in the sky before the destruction of Jerusalem. In speaking of medicine Isidore quotes the opinion of a certain physician that the physician should devote himself to the study of astronomy, because the human body changes with the mutations of the stars and seasons. In this same section Isidore discusses the various remedies in use among physicians, and though he is uncritical in his selection of material, yet, as O. Probst points out, he is free from all superstitious beliefs in the value of plants. Here again his scientific attitude is a clear condemnation of the idea that certain plants or potions had magical qualities. In speaking of the stars Isidore points out clearly the difference between "natural" and superstitious astrology. Natural astrology is concerned with the movement of the stars, and is practically synonymous with the modern term astronomy. Superstitious astrology teaches that man's birth and moral actions are dependent upon the motions of the stars. As Isidore devotes a small section of this work to magic, it may be well to summarize his discussion on this point.

He begins his treatment on this subject by asserting that it was introduced by the Persians and Assyrians. The spread and prevalence of magic throughout the world for so many centuries was due to the influence which the fallen angels exerted upon men. Isidore then proceeds to define various kinds of magic, such as necromancy, hydromancy, geomancy, aeromancy, and pyromancy. Under the heading of magic he also groups the practice of divination, by means of the flight of birds, the entrails of animals, and the movement of the stars. It is not at all improbable that Isidore in his discussion had in mind actual magical practices among the people of Spain, for, as has already been mentioned, magic and divination had been repeatedly condemned by the Church councils and also by the *Forum Iudicum*. In closing his treatment of magic, Isidore again stresses the connection between magic and demonology and condemns absolutely the practice of magic in any form. In view of the fact that this section on magic was copied by later mediaeval writers, it is quite probable that Isidore's condemnation of magic had a great influence upon the Visigothic clergy, and made them realize the necessity of combating all magical practices among the people.

In the *Etymologiae* Isidore emphasized, as Augustine before him, the allegorical interpretation of numbers: "We must not despise the science of numbers, for the deep significance which they have is evident from many passages of Holy Scripture." But nowhere in his writing does Isidore show any belief in the pagan superstition that certain numbers were either lucky or unlucky. Thorndike is rather severe in his judgment of Isidore's fondness for such allegorical interpretation of numbers: "With such mental magic and 'pious arithmetic,' as his friend Braulio called it, might the Christian sate the inherited thirst in him for the operative magic and pagan divination in which his conscience and his Church no longer allowed him to indulge."

Isidore's efforts to elevate the educational standards of the clergy were not limited to the composition of books. Many of the principles on education advocated in his writings were translated into legislation at the fourth Council of Toledo (633), over which he presided. The council declared that henceforth one "ignorant of letters" was not to be appointed bishop. In another canon the bishops stated that the *"sacerdotes"* should have a knowledge of Sacred Scripture and the canons (of the Church). The term *"sacerdotes"* here presumably includes priests as well as bishops. It is hardly probable that the council would insist *only* upon the bishops possessing this knowledge of the Scriptures and canons, since ordinarily the members of the hierarchy were selected from the ranks of the priests. Lest the priest should be ignorant of the ceremonies of the Church, the council ordered that each priest was to receive a manual containing the rubrics and prayers for the liturgical functions. This presentation of the manual formed a part of the ordination ceremony in the Mozarabic rite. With an eye to the future it was provided at this meeting that boys aspiring to the priesthood were henceforth to live together under the supervision of a learned and holy priest. While Spain may not have been the first nation in western

Europe to inaugurate these schools, the forerunners of the modern seminaries, there was no other region of Europe that insisted upon them so strongly in the seventh century. The effect of these salutary measures may be judged from the fact that the Isidorean tradition of scholarship was continued by men like Braulio, Ildefonse, Taio, Eugene and Julian, who were far superior in learning to the other contemporary ecclesiastics of western Europe.

A second indirect means that aided the struggle against paganism in Spain were the exorcisms and blessings in the Mozarabic rite. The purpose of the exorcisms was to free the people from the dread of the evil spirits, and to make them vividly conscious of the unity and power of God. The blessings served the purpose of supplanting pagan practices in vogue among some of the people of Spain. Hence in the following paragraphs attention will be drawn to some of the exorcisms and blessings of the Mozarabic rite that helped to counteract pagan beliefs and practices.

There was a special exorcism of the oil which was used as a remedy in time of sickness. In this exorcism the priest prayed that the oil might be a safeguard against the attacks of the devils, the arts of the Chaldeans, and the incantations of the augurs and diviners. A similar formula is found in an English liturgical book of the eleventh century, and may have been copied from the Visigothic liturgy. In the exorcism of the salt used in the blessing of a new home the priest besought God through the merits of Jesus to drive out the devil from whatever places the salt might touch. This formula is found in an eleventh century manuscript of the liturgy of Lyons. Doubtless this exorcism of the salt which was to be used in blessing the home helped to supplant the pagan "purification" ceremonies which Martin of Braga censured in his *Capitula.*

There are many blessings in the Mozarabic rite which concern farming, such as the blessing for new land which is to be broken, the planting of the seed, and the gathering of the first fruits and the harvests. These blessings, as Férotin remarks, are found in other liturgies besides the Mozarabic, but the formulas used in them are often peculiar to the Visigothic church. A prayer was said over the instrument used in pruning the vines and fruit trees, a blessing which is found only in the Mozarabic rite. In the blessing of a new well, the priest besought God to drive away from it every attack of the devil. A similar blessing is also found in the Sacramentary of Bobbio. This Christian blessing helped to counteract the pagan customs at the wells which Martin of Braga had censured in his sermon. On the occasion of a burial the priest recited a formula, found also in the Gelasian sacramentary, asking God to free this last resting-place from the attacks of the devil. Over the graves in Spain, as Férotin points out, a cross was placed. This blessing of the grave and the sight of the cross above it doubtless encouraged the people to be reconciled to the death of their loved ones, and to abandon all pagan practices at the tombs, which Martin of Braga had condemned. An unusual blessing which, as far as is known, is found nowhere else was that of the fisherman's net. In this prayer God was asked to preserve these nets from harm by diabolical enchantment and intervention. Férotin has remarked that the Spanish liturgy is very rich in prayers and blessings for those about to start on a journey. These prayers and blessings helped to drive out from the minds of the people the belief that certain days were unlucky and that no traveling should be done on them.

A very effective means of combating paganism, which continued for a long time in the country districts, was the establishment of rural parishes and monasteries. It is very probable that Christianity had penetrated into the country districts even before the Council of Elvira at the beginning of the fourth century. But during the long period of the Germanic invasions, when even fortified cities fell before the attacks of the barbarians, the majority of these simple and perishable country churches were doubtless either destroyed or left in ruins. After the conversion of the Sueves and Goths to Catholicism, however, there is mention in the Church councils of the churches built by the wealthy people of Spain. These churches, which were often erected on the large estates, ministered to the spiritual needs of the donor of the church and to the people of the surrounding country. By the year 633, when the fourth council of Toledo convened, these country churches had reached a high state of development. This is evident from the disputes which arose at the time between bishops who claimed jurisdiction over the same parish, or between the bishop and the person who had endowed the church.

The monastic form of life which had begun in Spain as early as the fourth century received a powerful impetus after the conversion of the Goths in 589. As there are only sparse records of the Visigothic period there were doubtless more than the twenty-seven monasteries, which are known to have existed. Some of the most distinguished churchmen of Visigothic Spain, such as Leander, John of Biclar, Julian, Ildefonse, Helladius, and John, the brother of Braulio, had formerly been monks. At the ninth council of Toledo in 655 there were present thirteen abbots. The Church councils not only gave their approval to the monastic life, but even allowed the bishops to aid financially in the erection of monasteries. As is evident from the rules of St. Isidore, and St. Fructuosus, the two most noted monastic legislators of Visigothic Spain, the monasteries were situated in the country sections. Usually churches were attached to the monasteries, and were frequented by the people of the neighborhood. As the hermit Valerius had destroyed the shrines of the idolatrous peasants, so the presence of the monks in the solitary regions doubtless did away with much idolatry. Mention has already been made of the fact that Bishop Masona had succeeded in converting many pagans by means of his charitable deeds; similarly the monasteries of Visigothic Spain, which were obliged to assist the poor, must have attracted to the Church many of the peasants who were still involved in the superstitious beliefs of pagan times.

The decline in the ecclesiastical discipline that was evident in the closing years of the seventh century in Spain must have hindered the development of the rural parishes and monasteries, and indirectly prevented the evangelization of the people of the country districts. It is significant that Egica in his address opening the sixteenth council of Toledo (693), which took action against the evil of idolatry, lamented the fact that many churches were without the services of priests and were in a dilapidated condition. Similarly the breakdown in the monastic discipline of Galicia is reflected in the writings of Valerius, who found the monks consorting with magicians and taking part in nocturnal meetings and dances in the forests. But the destruction of the Visigothic kingdom by the Arabs in 712, and the scarcity of source material for the history of Spain in the eighth and ninth centuries make it impossible to judge how general was this decline in the country parishes and monasteries of Spain.

CONCLUSION

The history of paganism in early Spain has been difficult to write because of the meagerness of the source material. For the most part only the merest gleanings of source material are extant. Thus, for example, the inscriptions in the pre-Christian period enable us to know the names of many of the gods worshiped in Spain, but tell us little or nothing of the religious rites performed in their honor. In the very important matter of the religion of the Germanic peoples who entered the Peninsula we have no means of knowing whether or not paganism was still deeply rooted among them. Early writers, both pagan and Christian, who have dealt with Spain say very little that is specific about paganism in the Peninsula. We are rather well informed, it is true, by a sermon of St. Martin of Braga about the pagan beliefs that flourished in Galicia in the sixth century, but we do not know whether the efforts of the saint were successful in suppressing them. Conciliar and civil legislation yields information only of a very general character contained as it is in prohibitions. Almost nothing remains to show us what success the measures taken against pagan survivals had attained as the Visigothic Kingdom drew to an end. Nevertheless in spite of these difficulties an analysis of the evidence presented in the preceding pages offers some interesting conclusions.

It is not until the Roman domination had been firmly established in Spain that we become acquainted through literary and epigraphical sources with the religion of the Peninsula. In this period the religious cults in Spain may be conveniently classified into two main divisions: those of the native population and those introduced by the Roman conquerors. The native cults predominated in western and northwestern Spain (modern Portugal and Galicia). In eastern and southern Spain, where the worship of the native gods had already disappeared at least by the time of the early empire, the Greco-Roman deities were worshiped by the natives as well as by the Romans, and there also the imperial cult attained its greatest popularity. The mystery religions of the empire were restricted mainly to the orientals who had settled in Spain and in the case of Mithraism to the soldiers stationed there.

The beginnings of Christianity in Spain are veiled in the greatest obscurity, and it is only at the Council of Elvira at the beginning of the fourth century that we have our first glimpse into the organization of the Spanish Church. By the beginning of the fourth century Christianity had become deeply rooted in the Romanized provinces of Baetica and Carthaginiensis and among its adherents were members of the Spanish aristocracy. Though the bishops at Elvira were uncompromising in their rejection of idolatry, they refrained from doing anything that might awaken the wrath of the civil authorities or arouse the pagan slaves to deeds of violence.

The Edict of Toleration, the gradual adoption of Christianity as the official religion of the State, and the anti-pagan legislation of the Christian emperors in the fourth century gave a death blow to the pagan religion of Rome. Pagan inscriptions in Spain, relatively so abundant in the first three centuries of the Christian Era, are seldom found there in the fourth century. But the prudence of the imperial authorities in refusing to allow the destruction of the pagan temples in Spain points to the fact that many people in the Peninsula were still attached to the old religion.

Christian Spain had escaped the harmful influences produced in other countries by the great Arian and Donatist heresies, but in the closing years of the fourth century it was troubled by the heresy of Priscillianism. This error included a considerable number of doctrines ultimately derived from paganism. The attempts of the ecclesiastical authorities to crush it at the first Council of Toledo increased the dissension in the Spanish Church, for some of the bishops of Baetica and Carthaginiensis refused to sanction the leniency of the council toward the Priscillianist bishops who had recanted their errors. It was not until the first Council of Braga in the second half of the sixth century that Priscillianism was suppressed.

The barbarian invasions of Spain in the opening years of the fifth century, which threw the whole Peninsula into confusion, had a marked influence upon the history of paganism. The Sueves were pagan upon their entry into Spain and doubtless many of the rank and file of the Arian Visigoths had but a thin veneer of Christianity. In the kingdom which the Sueves founded in Galicia in 464 Arianism was the State religion, and, as in Visigothic Spain during the Arian period, the rulers were out of sympathy with, if not openly antagonistic toward their Catholic subjects. Furthermore, there is nothing to indicate that the Arian bishops at this time were active in suppressing paganism. Hence during the fifth and the greater part of the sixth century the ecclesiastical authorities were greatly hampered in the evangelization of the people. It was only after the Sueves and Goths had embraced Catholicism that any successful efforts could be made against the paganism that still survived.

In Galicia the leading spirit in the struggle against paganism was St., Martin of Braga, the Apostle of the Sueves. As we learn from his *De correctione rusticorum* the paganism which Martin encountered in the country districts of Galicia consisted in magical beliefs and practices and the superstitious cult of trees, stones and fountains. St. Martin was relatively mild in his attitude towards those who practiced idolatry. Nowhere in his sermon does he advocate the use of physical punishment against idolaters. Paganism in his opinion was due not to malice, but to ignorance. He believed that once the people had become thoroughly acquainted with the teachings of their faith and the absurdity and sinfulness of paganism they would abandon their superstitious beliefs and practices. This mildness of the saint is in striking contrast to the severity which St. Caesarius of Arles, St. Eligius, and the civil and ecclesiastical authorities of Visigothic Spain showed toward idolaters.

In the Spanish kingdom of the Goths there is no such figure in the struggle against paganism as St. Martin of Braga. Among the Goths the leadership was in the hands of the councils and civil authorities. When the bishops of Spain met at the third council of Toledo (589) to celebrate the conversion of king Recared they realized that paganism was "deeply rooted throughout almost the whole of Spain." The council authorized the bishop and secular judge in their respective localities to punish idolaters and to destroy the places which were sacred in the eyes of the superstitious. The lack of source material in the period immediately following this council prevents us from knowing whether the council's efforts succeeded or failed. From the silence about this abuse at the fourth council of Toledo (633) it would seem that paganism was no longer regarded as a serious menace. For a slightly later date the Visigothic Code of civil law is an important source concerning the history of Spanish paganism. The survivals of paganism mentioned there are magic and divination. Corporal punishments, exile, and in some cases even death were the penalties meted out to magicians and diviners. This law code also reveals the primitive ideas about magical potions which still persisted in Spain.

The long reign of Receswinth, who promulgated this code, witnessed a noticeable decline in the organization of the Church, which seems to have led indirectly to the revival of pagan beliefs and practices among the people. At two of the national councils of Toledo in the closing years of the seventh century the bishops took action against those who worshiped at the sacred trees, stones and fountains. The measures which the councils ordered were severe physical punishments upon the offenders and heavy fines upon those who connived at their idolatry. During this period of decline there was also a revival of the pagan Germanic practice of the ordeal, which was legalized in what was probably the last law incorporated in the Visigothic Code.

This study has emphasized the indirect means made use of in Visigothic Spain in combating paganism: the education of the clergy, the exorcisms, and blessings of the Mozarabic rite, and the establishment of rural parishes and monasteries. The instruction of the clergy formed a notable part of the work of St. Isidore of Seville, and doubtless this education made the Spanish clergy better equipped to instruct the people and show them the folly and malice of paganism. The exorcisms and prayers of the Spanish Church supplanted and counteracted pagan practices and customs which survived among the people. The establishment of parish churches and monasteries in rural districts, which followed the restoration of Spain to religious unity in 589, brought the influence of Christianity closer to the peasants among whom paganism had cast the deepest roots.

From an examination of all the available evidence it is possible to draw some definite conclusions about the types of paganism that survived in Spain, the localities in which paganism flourished, the classes of people who were guilty of superstitious practices, and the means used to combat paganism.

In the period of which we have been treating the two principal forms of pagansim that survived were the cult of trees, stones and fountains and the practice of magic and divination. "Sacred" trees, stones and fountains were still the centers of superstitious worship in the sixth and seventh centuries as they had been in pre-Christian times. Magic and divination were particularly difficult to eradicate.

Priscillianism inculcated among the people a belief in the efficacy of magic and astrology. St. Martin of Braga in the sixth century found the peasants of Galicia pronouncing incantations over herbs, and seeking by superstitious means to divine the future. The Visigothic Code and the acts of the councils contain a number of laws against the practice of magic and divination.

If we examine the history of paganism in Spain from a geographical standpoint we find that pagan beliefs and practices were strongest in Galicia. The evidence brought forward in the first chapter shows quite clearly that the native deities were especially popular among the people of that region. In the fourth century, when Christianity was already in a flourishing condition throughout southern and eastern Spain, it had merely penetrated into the cities of northwestern Spain. Moreover Priscillianism with its pagan beliefs and practices had been popular among the people of Galicia, and for almost a hundred years (464-550), Arianism had been the predominant religion in the Suevian kingdom. Hence it is not surprising that St. Martin in the sixth century found paganism very rife among the peasants, whose religious instruction had been so much neglected. In this same section of Spain in the closing years of the Visigothic kingdom St. Valerius also found evidences of paganism among the people. In other parts of Spain paganism did not disappear entirely with the coming of Christianity. St. Pacianus in the last quarter of the fourth century found many pagan practices in vogue among the people of Barcelona. The third council of Toledo (589) realized that the long period of time during which the Arians had been predominant in Spain had led to the spread of paganism. Later on in the middle of the seventh century, when a marked decline had taken place in the ecclesiastical discipline, two of the national councils called attention to the growing evil of idolatry and superstition. The severity which these councils showed towards idolaters and the threat of removing from office any bishop or judge negligent in prosecuting idolaters would seem to indicate that paganism was widespread in the Peninsula.

In Spain as elsewhere paganism continued longest in the country districts. This is evident from the works of St. Pacianus in the fourth century, from the sermon of St. Martin of Braga in the sixth century, and from the writings of St. Valerius and the conciliar legislation of the seventh century. In the closing years of the Visigothic kingdom the canons on paganism show that superstition was very prevalent among the slaves. At two of the Spanish councils in the seventh century the bishops deemed it necessary to punish clerics found guilty of consulting magicians and diviners and those priests who practiced magic rites themselves.

We are rather well informed about the means adopted to suppress paganism in Visigothic Spain and in Galicia. In Visigothic Spain the means most often used against idolaters were civil penalties, and as a rule corporal punishment, though in punishing magicians the Visigothic Code was not as harsh as the Theodosian Code. St. Martin of Braga, as has already been pointed out, followed a policy of mildness. He did not sanction the use of force in the suppression of idolatry, and emphasized the necessity of religious instruction. Which of these two methods proved more successful in practice is difficult to determine. Little is known about the history of Galicia in the period subsequent to Martin's death, while the lack of contemporary documents in Spain for the period immediately after the Moorish conquest makes it impossible to draw any definite conclusions about the survivals of ancient paganism.

www.ingramcontent.com/pod-product-compliance
Lightning Source LLC
Chambersburg PA
CBHW051735090426

42738CB00010B/2260